BIHAR :
A SELECT BIBLIOGRAPHY 1962-1975

BIHAR :
A SELECT BIBLIOGRAPHY
1962-1975

Compiled and Edited by
SATYAPRAKASH

GURGAON / NEW DELHI
INDIAN DOCUMENTATION SERVICE

Indian States Bibliography Series—3

FIRST PUBLISHED 1976
BY INDIAN DOCUMENTATION SERVICE,
GURGAON, HARYANA 122 001 &
2, DARYAGANJ, ANSARI ROAD, PANNA BHAWAN,
NEW DELHI 110 002 INDIA
SET IN 10 POINT BASKERVILLE ROMAN
AND PRINTED IN INDIA BY THE ACADEMIC PRESS,
GURGAON, HARYANA 122 001

PREFACE

This bibliography on Bihar indexes 2,536 articles, research papers, notes, book reviews, news - both national and regional, editorials and signed articles published in selected 113 Indian English language journals and the daily *Times of India* through the fourteen-year period 1962-1975. About 100 independent books in all languages on different facets of Bihar have also been included in the book and distinguished by a star (*). A complete list of journals indexed, with their abbreviations, and a list of the book publishers have also been given to facilitate the readers in obtaining material.

The material has been classified and arranged on the dictionary pattern by authors and subjects in an alphabetical sequence, with a view to provide a most easy form of consultation.

The volume has been styled *Indian States Bibliography Series—3*. We are publishing independent volumes on all the Indian States and Union Territories and a number of them are under preparation or in the printing process.

We are far from perfection. It is a very modest attempt to encompass the entire mass of material on Bihar published in the Indian Press. I hope our efforts, though meagre, will be useful to the students, researchers, historians and the journalists studying life and progress of Bihar. Readers' critical evaluation and their suggestions for improvements in future editions of the bibliography are welcome.

Gurgaon,   Satyaprakash
June 23, 1976.

BIHAR
A SELECT BIBLIOGRAPHY
1962-1975

GENERAL

*Bihar. Mohanlal Viyogi Mahati. Rajhans. 1960, 46p. Rs 1.75

Bihar : The land and the people. *ill Wkly India* 89(11) 17 Mr'68 8-13 ills

Introducing India-12 : Bihar. Deoki Nandan Singh *ill Wkly India* 88(40) 5 Nv'67 28-31 ills

The problem of self-renewal in Bihar. Jayaprakash Narayan *Commerce (Suppl)* 127(3263) 17 Nv'73 3-5

ABDUL GHAFOOR
Bihar : An uphill task. *Link* 16(25) 26 Ja'74 35-37

ADITYA NARAIAN, Lala
A study in the techniques of the neolithicbone tool making at Chirand and their probable uses. *J Bihar Res Soc* 58(1-4) Ja-De'72 1-24 figs bibliogr

ADMINISTRATIVE Courts
Administrative tribunals in action—A study of administrative tribunals at the district level in Bihar. Vishnu Prasad. Oxf-IBH. vii, 240p. Rs 32 Review
Commerce 130(3340) 24 My'75 793

ADULT education
Pilot literacy project in Bihar. M.R.N. Sharma *Indian J Adult Educ* 28(3) Mr'67 16

AGARWAL, Jagannath
Some observations on the Bihar stone pillar inscription. *J orient Inst* 20(1) Se'70 44-47 bibliogr-ft-n

AGRAWAL, N.C.

Handloom industry of Manpur (Gaya) : A survey. *Indian J Commerce* 23(3) Se'70 87-95

AGRICULTURAL cooperative credit societies

Provision of credit and supplies : A case study in Shahabad district. J.S. Chawhan *Indian Cooperative Rev* 2(4) Jl'65 563-73 tabs

Some aspects of agricultural credit cooperatives in Bihar. B.D. Sharma *Indian Cooperative Rev* 7(3) Ap'70 428-32

AGRICULTURAL credit

Agriculture in Bihar and the nationalised commercial banks. Rajkishore Sinha *Bihar Inform* 18(10) 1 Je'70 5-6 bibliogr-ft-n

Confusing picture of agricultural financing. *Commerce* 119(3060) 27 De'69 1235

Hurdles to flow of farm credit through co-operatives in Bihar. B.D. Sharma *Southern Econ* 10(15) 1 De'71 27-28

Planning and implementation of financing agriculture through area approach. (A case study of Bihar State). D.K. Desai and Hari Prakash. IIM. 1973, 148p. Rs 7
Review
Indian J agric Econ 28(3) Jl-Se'73 83-86

Planning and implementation of financing the area development scheme. D.K. Desai and Hari Prakash *econ and Political Wkly (Suppl)* 7(31) 25 Mr'72 A-13-A-22 tabs ft-n

Provision of credit and supplies : A case study in Shahabad district. J.S. Chawhan *Indian Cooperative Rev* 2(4) Jl'65 563-73 tabs

Short-term credit and farm productivity in an I.A.D.P. district. Dru Srivastava and others *Kurukshetra* 18(2) Nv'69 5-6

See also

Mortgage banks

AGRICULTURAL economics

Change in the pattern of capital formation in agriculture. Gyaneshwar Ojha *Indian J agric Econ* 24(4) Oc-De'69 138-39

Investment of farm and capital formation in agriculture in Bihar. S.N. Sen *Indian J agric Econ* 20(1) Ja-Mr'65 163-66 tab

Investment on farm and capital formation in agriculture

with particular reference to Bihar. C.P. Shastri *Indian J agric Econ* 20(1) Ja-Mr'65 174-83 tabs

Land tenure system and capital formation in agriculture. D. Jha and S.D. Salunke *Indian J agric Econ* 24(4) Oc-De'69 130-31

Monghyr Agricultural Production Conference. Ali Ashraf *New Age* 11(17) 28 Ap'63 14

Peep into productivity in Bihar. B.N. Sahu *Productivity* 6(2-3) 1965 368-69

*Silent revolution; a report of the second All-Chotanagpur Seminar held at Samtoli, December, 1969. Vikas Maitri. 1970, 52p.

AGRICULTURAL education

Bihar ushers in Rajendra Agricultural University. S.K. Mukerji *Indian Fmg* 20(11) Fe'71 33-36

AGRICULTURAL extension work

Agricultural extension programme : How rural leaders and followers look at it. N.K. Jaiswal and others *quart J Local Self-Government Inst* 42(1) Jl-Se'71 63-72 tabs

Comparative analysis of role expectations and role performances of subject matter specialists in package and non-package districts. A.K. Singh and R.P. Singh *Indian J Adult Educ* 34(6) Je'73 11-13 tabs

AGRICULTURAL industries

Scope for agro-based industries. P.N. Sinha *Commerce (Suppl)* 127(3263) 17 Nv'73 27-29

AGRICULTURAL labourers

Agricultural labour in Bihar. Girish Mishra *mod Rev* 118(4) Oc'65 312-20

Agricultural labourers demand minimum wages. *New Age* 12(31) 2 Ag'64 15

Agricultural workers' struggle. Jagannath Sarkar *New Age* 12(34) 23 Ag'64 2

_____ : Employment

Rural labour market (based on a study conducted in the district of Darbhanga, Bihar 1954-64). S.N. Thakur *Indian J agric Econ* 25(3) Jl-Se'70 65-66

Structure, employment and earnings of agricultural labour in Champaran district in Bihar. D. Jha *Indian J agric Econ* 25(3) Jl-Se'70 64-65

AGRICULTURAL policy
  See Agriculture and state

AGRICULTURAL wages

Factors determining agricultural wages : A case study. M.L. Singh and K.K. Singh *Indian J agric Econ* 29(3) Jl-Se'74 54-60 tabs bibliogr-ft-n

Minimum wages. *econ and Political Wkly* 10(29) 19 Jl'75 1076

A study of the level of real earnings of agricultural workers in Bihar 1961-70. S.P. Sinha and B.N. Verma *Indian J agric Econ* 29(3) Jl-Se'74 70-71

AGRICULTURE

Agrarian condition in Kosi project area. *People's Democracy* 5(42) 19 Oc'69 4+

Agriculture in Bihar : Growth rate in rice production has not kept pace with other cereals and pulses. M.P. Pandey *Yojana* 19(10) 15 Je'75 35-36

Changing agricultural income in Bihar. Manju Sinha *Commerce (Suppl)* 127(3263) 17 Nv'73 75-76

The changing face of Bihar agriculture. S.R. Bose *Indian J agric Econ* 51(2) Oc'70 169-84 tabs

The disaster that never was. *Productivity* 9(2) 1968 12-13

Green revolution in Bihar. Wolf Ladejinskly *econ and Political Wkly (Suppl)* 43(9) 23 Se'69 A-147-A-62 bibliogr-ft-n

Kurwa : The shifting cultivation of the Maler. Saileshwar Prasad *Vanyajati* 19(2-3) Ap-Jl'71 95-100 bibliogr

Nature and role of the risk and uncertainty in agricultural production in Bihar. S.N. Sen *Indian J agric Econ* 19(1) Ja-Mr'64 107-09

A new revolution in Champaran. *Kurukshetra* 19(20) 16 Jl'71 11-12

Planning and agricultural development. D.N. Jha. S. Chand. 1974, 232p. Rs 30 Review *Indian J industr Relations* 10(4) Ap'75 615-17

Prospects of commercial crops better. *Bihar Inform* 16(20) 1 De'68 4-5

Social dimensions of agricultural development. Sachchidananda. National Pub H. 1972, 195p. Rs 30 Review *Behavioural Sci and Community Development* 7(1) Mr'73 74-77; *soc Action* 23(1) Ja-Mr'73 110-11

The state of agriculture-3, Bihar : Dependence on monsoon. *Commerce (Annual Number)* 115(2956) 1967 140-41 tabs

A study in Bihar agriculture. S.R. Bose. Sinha Inst of Soc Stud. 1967, 61p. Review
Indian J Agric Econ 23(1) Ja-Mr'68 89

A study of agricultural production pattern in Bihar (**A** demand and supply analysis). S.P. Sinha and Biony Nath Verma *Indian J agric Econ* 27(4) Oc-De'72 143-46 tabs

Vaishali blazes a trail again. B.P. Chaturvedi *Bihar Inform* 18(21) 16 De'70 1+

Wheat revolution in Shahabad. J.N. Sinha *Bihar Inform* 18(16) 16 Se'70 4-5 Repr

    See also
Irrigation

AGRICULTURE and state

Under Bihar united front : Struggle for agrarian reforms. Indradeep Sinha *Mainstream* 6(25) 17 Fe'68 10-15

AHMAD, E.

Geography of Ranchi university. *Geographical Rev India* 33(1) Mr'68 33-40 tabs bibliogr

AHUJA, Ram

Political elites and modernisation. Meenakshi. Rs 30 Review
TI 17 Ag'75 6 : 1-3

AIYAR, Swaminathan S.

Assent to Bill on abolition of Tata zamindari withheld. *TI* 26 Oc'71 1 : 7-8+

AJTEKAR, Anant Sadasiv and Misra, Vijaykant

*Report on Kumrahar excavations, 1951-1955. K.P. Jayaswal Res Inst. (Historical research series). Vol 3. 1959, xvi, 142p. Rs 40

AKHTAR, H.S.M.Q. and others

Attitudes and practices of graduate school teachers towards family planning. *J Family Welfare* 19(1) Se'72 57-65 tabs bibliogr

ALAM, S. Sanjar F. and others

Attitude of tribals and non-tribals of Ranchi towards fertilizers. *Man in India* 52(4) Oc-De'72 328-34 tabs

ALI ASHRAF

Bihar-Communists double seats. *New Age* 10(10) 11 Mr'622

Growing unity against right reaction. *New Age* 11(5) 3 Fe'63 4+

Monghyr Agricultural Production Conference. *New Age* 11(17) 28 Ap'63 14

Open struggle to topple Jha ministry. *New Age* 11(13) 31 Mr'63 6

Vitiated atmosphere in group policies. *New Age* 11(14) 7 Ap'63 6

ALL India Kisan Sabha : Bihar unit

Bihar Kisan conference charts six-point demand. *New Age* 12(22) 31 My'64 7

ALL India Trade Union Congress : Bihar unit

B.P.T.U.C. special convention : Pleads to increase production. Ajoy Dasgupta *New Age* 11(1) 6 Ja'63 15

AMAR SINGH

*Economic classification of state government budgets in India, 1958-59. Panjab Univ. (Dept. of Economics). 1958, ii, 26p. 24cm.

AMBASTHA, A.V.

Sugar industry in Bihar. *AICC econ Rev* 20(1) 15 Jl'68 7-10 tabs

AMBASTHA, C K.

See Jaiswal, N.K. jt. auth.; Singh, R.P. jt. auth.

_____ and Das, B.N.

Marketing of jute in Madhipura mandi of Saharsa district in Bihar. *Bihar Inform* 18(19) 16 Nv'70 13-14

_____ and Jaiswal, N.K.

Manpower-utilisation in east Bihar villages. *Rural India* 32(11) Nv'69 273-75 tab

AMES, Michael M.

Modernisation and social structure : Family caste and class in Jamshedpur. *econ and Political Wkly* 4(28-30) Jl'69 121-24 tab

ANANTHASAYANAM AYYANGAR, M.

Administration of a state as seen by a Governor. *Eastern Econ* 52(16) 18 Ap'69 814-18

ANIL KUMAR

See Singh, R.P. jt. auth.

ANIMAL Husbandry

*Animal production in Bihar. Muhammad Fahim-ud-Din,

Asia. 1963, xii, 166p. pls maps tabs bibliogr 24.5cm. Rs 18.50

ANSARI, Hasan Nishat

Historical geography of Bihar on the eve of the early Turkish invasions. *J Bihar Res Soc* 49(1-4) Ja-De'63 253-60

Tirhut (North Bihar) and Bihar (South Bihar) under Muhammad Tughluq—A.D. 1325-1351. *J Bihar Res Soc* 50(1-4) Ja-De'64 59-72 bibliogr

ANTHROPOGEOGRAPHY

*The Asur, a study of primitive ironsmelters. K.K. Leuva. Bharatiya Adimjati Sevak Sangh. 1963, xviii, 234p. pls bibliogr 22.5cm. Rs 17.50

ANTIQUITIES

*Antiquities of Belgam and Kaladgi. James Burgess. Indological bk House. 46p. 56 pls Rs 100

The archaeology of Bihar. Parmeshwari Lal Gupta *Bihar Inform* 18(2) 26 Ja'70 1-3

Material culture of chalcolithic Bihar. Bhagwant Sahai *J Bihar Res Soc* 58(1-4) Ja-De'72 1-24 figs bibliogr

ARCHAEOLOGY

*Report of the first season's operations in the Belgam and Kaladgi district, January to May 1874. James Burgess. Indological bk House. 45, 56p. Rs 100

ARCHER, Mildred

Bazaar style. *Marg* 20(1) De'66 53-54

ARCHITECTURE, Mohammedan

The Indo-Islamic architecture of Bihar. Z.A. Desai *Islamic Cult* 46(1) Ja'72 17-38

ARCHIVES

A note on historical records and state central archives in Bihar. K.K. Datta *Indian Arch* 15 Ja'63-De'64 1-7

ART

*Bharatiya kala ko Bihar ki den. Vindhyesvariprasad Simha. Bihar Rashtrabhasha Parishad. (H). 1958, xx, 203p. pls

ASURS

Impact of community development on a tribal community. P.C. Roy Choudhury *Khadi Gramodyog* 13(9) Je'67 657-60

BAGCHI, K. and Sen, U.
Giridih : Its growth and land use. *Geographical Rev India*
24(4) De'63 243-50

BAITHA, Narsingh
Irrigation in Bihar. *Bihar Inform* 18(11) 16 Je'70 3-4

BALBIR DUTT
Four crore people of Bihar on the brink of starvation.
Organiser 27(38) 27 Ap'74 13

BALCHAND, R.
Rise and fall of the Vrijjian Republic. *Bihar Inform* 18(2)
26 Ja'70 4-8

BANDYOPADHYAY, Suraj
See Chattopadhyay, Kumarananda jt. auth.

BANERJEE, Maya
Literacy in Singhbhum, Bihar. *Geographical Rev India* 37(2)
Je'75 151-57 tabs bibliogr

BANERJEE, Shailendra Nath
Effect of changes in age-patterns of marriage on fertility
rates in Bihar, 1961-86. *Man in India* 53(3) Jl-Se'73 262-78
tabs bibliogr

BANERJI, Adris
Some post-Muslim temples of Bihar. *J Asiatic Soc (Bengal)*
4(2) 1962 63-70 pls.

An unfinished rekha deal of Purulia. *J Asiatic Soc (Bengal)*
7(3-4) 1965 163-66 bibliogr-ft-n

BANKS and banking
Banking by State Government. Indra Kumar *Mankind*
13(1) Ja-Fe'69 31-32

See also

Mortgage banks

BARAUNI
Administrative precinct, Barauni. *Indian Architect* 8(1)
Ja'66 6-11 figs

Housing Barauni. *Indian Architect* 8(1) Ja'66 12-14 figs

Oil town at Barauni, Bihar. *Indian Architect* 8(1) Ja'66 3-6

BARUA, Dipak Kumar
Vikramasila monastery—An ancient seat of learning. *Maha
Bodhi* 75(5-6) My-Je'67 204-05

BASU, Ashish
 Hill area crafts in Darjeeling. *Khadi Gramodyog* 13(4)
 Ja'67 347-50

BASU, Tridib Kumar
 Functional classification of urban settlement in Singbhum
 district, Bihar : A cartographical appraisal. *Geographical
 Rev India* 37(2) Je'75 165-71 tabs bibliogr appdx

BEETS and beet sugar
 Problems and possibilities of growing sugarbeet in Bihar.
 A.K. Singh *Farmer and Parliament* 9(3) Mr'74 7-8+ tabs

BEGGING
 The beggar problem in Ranchi. T.S. Rao and M.V.D.
 Bogaert *Indian J soc Wk* 31(3) Oc'70 285-302 tabs
 bibliogr-ft-n appdx

BEY, Hamdi
 Small town stories. Barua Agency. Rs 22 Review
 TI 30 Mr'75 8 : 4-5

BHAGVANCANDRA, Vinod
 *Kar bhala hoga bhala. Sasta Sahitya Mandal. 1960.

BHAGWANT SAHAI
 An interesting stone panel from the Visnupada temple. *J
 Ganganath Jha Res Inst* 26(1-3) Ja-Jl'70 709-15 bibliogr-ft-n

BHARATIYA Kranti Dal : Bihar unit
 BKD is just like KMPP. *Organiser* 21(15) 19 Nv'67 1+

 Bharatiya Kranti Dal : Kabir's shadow. *Link* 10(21)
 31 De'67 9-10

 Bihar BKD group replaces. M.P. Sinha *TI* 2 Mr'69 9 : 4

 Dissidents as partners. *econ and Political Wkly* 2(46)
 25 Nv'67 2045-46

 Kabir disruption. *Link* 10(7) 24 Se'67 17

 Kranti Dal needs clarity. *New Age* 15(21) 21 Mr'67 2

 Left of the centre party. *Commerce* 114(2923) 20 My'67
 872

 Poor start. *Link* 10(12) 29 Oc'67 10+

 Rebel Congressmen's party. *Link* 9(41) 21 My'67 10-14
 ills pors

 Rightist success. *Link* 10(9) 8 Oc'67 11

 Rival to Bangla Congress. *Link* 10(6) 17 Se'67 16-17

 Search for indentity. *Link* 10(15) 19 Nv'67 21

Snub for Kabir : Kranti Dal firmly against topple plots.
L.R. Khandkar *New Age* 15(47) 19 Nv'67 7

BHARDVAJ, Laksmanprasad
*Pataliputra. Yaspal Jain, *ed.* Sasta Sahitya Mandal. (H).
1959, 30p. ills 18cm. Re 0.37

BHARGAVA, B.S.
Panchayats in Bihar : A critical study. *mod Rev* 120(2)
Ag'66 140-47

BHARGAVA, P.N. and others
Study of marketable surplus of paddy in Shahabad district.
econ Affairs 20(1-2) Ja-Fe'75 56-64 tabs bibliogr

BHASIN, Prem
The mood of the moment. *Janata* 29(41) 24 Nv'74 7-9

The significance of Bihar. *Janata* 29(28) 15 Ag'74 33-35

BHATIA, Sudarshan
Front bid to defeat. Jagjivan Ram *TI* 19 Fe'71 7 : 1-2

Most parties are faced with internal quarrels. *TI* 16 Fe'71
5 : 4-5

BHATNAGAR, J.P.
*Commentary on the Law of Excise in Bihar and Orissa.
Ashoka Law H. 282p. Rs 12.50

BHATTACHARJEA, Ajit
Despair and hope in Bihar : An end and a beginning. *TI*
17 Se'73 4 : 3-5; 18 Se'73 4 : 3-5

JP's expanding objective : Reaction to Congress cynicism.
TI 18 Je'74 4 : 3-5

What's going on in Bihar. *ill Wkly India* 95(21) 21 Jl'74 4-9

BHATTACHARYYA, R. and Sen, U.
Rajgir and its surroundings. *Geographical Rev India* 28(2)
Je'66 41-46

BHATTACHARYYA, Subhendu Sekhar
Woodland verses. *Bull Cult Res Inst* 3(3-4) 1964 49-64

BHUMJI
Space, time and ethnicity : Field study among the Bhumji
of Barabhum. Surajit Sinha *J Indian anthrop Soc* 9(2)
Oc'74 155-62 bibliogr

BIHAR Alloy Steels Ltd.
Alloy steels in Bihar; editorial. *Eastern Econ* 58(8) 25 Fe'72
293-94

BIHAR State Agro-Industries Development Corporation Ltd.
Bihar State Agro-Industries Development Corporation. U.N. Sinha *Commerce (Suppl)* 127(3263) 17 Nv'73 63-67

BIHAR State Financial Corporation
Bihar State Financial Corporation; speech by the Chairman, Ambika Sharan Singh, at the 18th annual g.m. held on 30 June, 1973, at Patna. *Commerce* 127(3257) 6 Oc'73 616-17+

BIHAR University
Anatomy of University in Bihar. A.P. Sharma *Mainstream* 7(27) 8 Mr'69 35-36

*Bihar University calendar (1956-58). Patna Univ. 1958.

Commission on Bihar University. *Link* 7(44) 13 Je'65 43-44

BIRSA
Birsa Bhagwan : The patriot. S.P. Sinha *Bihar Inform* 18(14) 15 Ag'70 38-40

BISWAS, M.K.
Socialism and non-congressism. *Janata* 23(46) 15 De'68 4

BLOCK development Officers
Profession of farming and service in agriculture department; as block personnel see them. R.P. Singh and C.K. Ambastha *Bihar Inform* 18(11) 16 Je'70 16-20 tabs

BOGAERT, M.V.D.
See Rao, T.S. jt. auth.

BOSE, S.R.
*Bihar population problems. Patna, A.N. Sinha Inst of Soc Stud. 87p.

The changing face of Bihar agriculture. *Indian J Econ* 51(2) Oc'70 169-84

A study in Bihar agriculture. A.N. Sinha Inst of Soc Stud. 1967, 61p. Review
Indian J agric Econ 23(1) Ja-Mr'68 89

BOSE, Sailesh Kumar
Tenurial reform in Bihar. *econ Stud* 4(6) De'63 291-96+

BOSE, Saroj Ranjan
*Study in Bihar agriculture. Mukhopadhyay. 1967, 61p. Rs 5

BOUNDARIES
U.P.-Bihar permanent boundary soon. *TI* 1 My'70 5 : 2-3

BRAHMANAND

JP's movement : A positive role to play. *Janata* 29(28) 15 Ag'74 27-29

BRIDGES

The Sone bridge. *Link* 8(16) 28 Nv'75 15

BUDGET

Bihar budget demands approved. *TI* 26 Je'69 1 : 6+

Bihar budget. *Eastern Econ* 46(6) 11 Fe'66 232

Bihar budget. *Eastern Econ* 51(7) 16 Ag'68 370

Bihar. *Eastern Econ* 56(13) 26 Mr'71 520

Bihar's budget. *Indian Fin* 91(10) 17 Mr'73 255

C.M. presents Rs 25.34 crore deficit budget; no fresh taxes levied. *Bihar Inform* 18(6) 1 Ap'70 2-4

Caught on wrong foot. *Commerce* 115(2931) 15 Jl'67 119+

A deficit budget for Bihar. *Capital* 154(3847) 11 Fe'65 191-92

A deficit budget for Bihar. *Commerce* 116(2968) 23 Mr'68 766-67

*Economic classification of state government budgets in India, 1958-59. Amar Singh. Panjab Univ (Dept. of Economics). 1958, ii, 26p. 24cm.

Feeble attempts to bridge budget deficit. *Commerce* 128(3281) 23 Mr'74 406

Fountainpens. *Link* 6(34) 5 Ap'64 14-15

Grave financial situation. *Commerce* 118(3023) 12 Ap'69 693

No new taxes in Bihar budget. *Eastern Econ* 44(6) 5 Fe'65 268-69

Rs 5.5 crores new taxes in Bihar : Mass protest before Assembly on March 1 planned. K. Gopalan *New Age* 14(8) 20 Fe'66 6

Rs 25-crores deficit in Bihar budget : No new taxes proposed. *TI* 17 Mr'70 5 : 2-3

Rs 31.14 crores deficit budget for Bihar. *Bihar Inform* 16(6) 1 Ag'68 3-4+

The search for funds. *Eastern Econ* 42(9) 29 Fe'64 384-87

State budgets : Bihar. *Commerce* 115(2930) 8 Jl'67 61

State budgets : Bihar. *Eastern Econ* 49(2) 14 Jl'67 80

State budgets of Bihar and Andhra. *Capital* 152(3799) 27 Fe'64   283-84

Taxes and evasion. *Link* 12(41) 24 My'70 17-18

Towards a balanced budget. *Commerce* 117(2989) 17 Ag'68 363

U P. and Bihar budgets. *Commerce* 110(2808) 20 Fe'65 278

Uneconomic holdings to be taxed in Bihar. *TI* 6 Mr'73 1 : 1-2+

BURGESS, James

*Antiquities of Belgam and Kaladgi. Indological bk House. 46p. 56 pls Rs 100

*Report of the first season's operations in the Belgam and Kaladgi district, January to May 1874. Indological bk House. 45, 56p. Rs 100

CARDING, Jane

Thoughts on Bihar. *ill Wkly India* 88(30) 27 Ap'67 16-17

CASTE

Caste and conflict in a Bihar village. Sachchidananda *Eastern Anthropologist* 20(2) My-Ag'67 143-50 bibliogr

Caste and occupation in a village in Bihar. K.N. Sahay *Man in India* 47(3) Jl-Se'67 178-88 bibliogr-ft-n

Caste and occupational mobility in two industrial towns of Bihar. B.B. Mandal *J soc Res* 16(1) Mr'73 59-64 tabs bibliogr-ft-n

Caste and occupational preference in East Bihar villages. N.K. Jaiswal and C.K. Ambastha *Indian J soc Wk* 31(2) Jl'70 191-95 tabs

Caste tension in Patna. Sachchidananda and K. Gopal Iyer *Eastern Anthropologist* 22(3) Se-De'69 327-48 tabs bibliogr

A comparative study on taste-blindness among the caste groups of West Bengal and Munda and Oraon of Ranchi, Bihar. Balaram De *Bull Cult Res Inst* 9(1-2) 1972 82-83 tabs bibliogr

Distribution of castes and search for a new theory of caste ranking : Case of the Saran plain. P.B. Singh *nat Geographical J India* 21(1) Mr'75 20-46 tabs figs bibliogr-ft-n

Many faces of caste politics. N.K. Singh *econ and Political Wkly* 7(15) 8 Ap'72 748-49

CASTE and politics

Caste in Bihar politics. Nagesh Jha *econ and Political Wkly* 5(7) 14 Fe'70 341-44 tabs

CHALAPATI RAO, C.

HEC marches ahead. *Bihar Inform* 17(15) 1 Se'69 18+; *Indian Fin* 84(7) 16 Ag'69 192

H.E.C.'s role in setting up the Bokaro Steel Plant. *Capital (Suppl)* 163(4070) 10 Jl'69 87-88

CHANDHOKE, S.K.

The Tana Bhagats of Chotanagpur. *Vanyajati* 20(3-4) Jl-Oc'72 128-44 bibliogr

The Tana Bhagats. *Vanyajati* 19(2-3) Ap-Jl'71 81-94 bibliogr

CHARLEY, Ganesh

See Vidyarathi, L.P. jt. auth.

CHATTERJEE, Rama

Members of medieval Brahmana family ruling in Gaya and their religious activities. *J Asiatic Soc (Bengal)* 7(1-2) 1965 7-11 bibliogr-ft-n

CHATTOPADHYAY, Kumarananda

Rites and rituals : Media of rural integration. *Eastern Anthropologist* 23(3) Se-De'70 217-33 tabs bibliogr

_____ and Bandyopadhyay, Suraj

Notes on a method of studying rural society. *Man in India* 42(3) Jl-Se'62 206-16 bibliogr-ft-n tabs

CHATURVEDI, B.P.

Vaishali blazes a trail again. *Bihar Inform* 18(21) 16 De'70 1+

CHAUBEY, U.D.

Urban water supply in Bihar through five-year plan. *Bihar Inform* 17(16) 16 Se'69 5-7

CHAUDHARY, Pawan

How to curb election expenses. *TI* 17 Oc'71 8 : 6-7

CHAUDHURI, Radhakrishna

*History of Bihar. Shanti Devi. 1958, x, 421p. Rs 12.50

The Khandavalas of Mithila. *J Bihar Res Soc (Sec II)* 48 Ja-De'62 41-63

*Select inscriptions of Bihar. Shanti Devi. 1958, 54, 138p. 18cm. Rs 10.50

CHAWHAN, J.S.

Provision of credit and supplies : A case study in Shahabad district. *Indian Cooperative Rev* 2(4) Jl'65 563-73 tabs

CHIEF Ministers

Abdul Ghafoor to be sworn in as Bihar C.M. today. *TI* 2 Jl'73 1 : 1-3

Challenge in Bihar; editorial. *TI* 8 Ap'75 4 : 1

Mrs Gandhi still undecided about new Bihar leader. *TI* 1 Jl'73 1 : 7-8+

Harihar Singh sworn in as Bihar C.M. *TI* 27 Fe'69 I : 4+

Pande bows out : Mishra is choice. *TI* 5 Ap'75 1 : 6+

Political circles hail Ghafoor's selection. *TI* 2 Jl'73 1 : 1-2+

Unanimous choice of Dr. Mishra likely. *TI* 4 Ap'75 1 : 4-5+

　　See also

Mishra, J.N.

Sahay, K.B.

Sinha, Mahamaya Prasad

CHOTA NAGPUR

Chota Nagpur is fast becoming another Nagaland. *Organiser* 21(40) 12 My'68 3

Chota Nagpur survey. F. Ivern. Indian Soc Inst. 1969, iv, 524p. Rs 36; $ 7.50 Review *soc Action* 20(3) Jl-Se'70 317-18

CHOUDHARY, Adhay Kant

The Mandar hill : A general survey. *J Bihar Res Soc* 50(1-4) Ja-De'64 32-42 bibliogr

CHOUHAN, K.N.K.

　　See Jaiswal, N.K. jt. auth.

CITIES and towns

Function and functional classification of towns in Bihar. Mahamaya Mukherji *Deccan Geographer* 8(1-2) Ja-De'70 56-66 tabs maps bibliogr-ft-n

Giridih : Its growth and land use. K. Bagchi and U. Sen *Geographical Rev India* 24(4) De'63 243-50

Need for functional classification of towns. Mahamaya Mukherji *Patna Univ J* 23(1) Ja'68 60-70 bibliogr-ft-n

Transport towns of Bihar. Mahamaya Mukherji *Indian Geographical J* 44(3-4) Jl-Se-Oc'69 42-51 tabs map bibliogr-ft-n

See also

Jamshedpur

Rajgir

CITY planning
See also

Barauni

COAL miners

Bihar miners gain assurance on bonus. K. Gopalan *New Age* 13(15) 11 Ap'65 6

Coal miners win bonus, more struggles ahead. *New Age* 14(17) 24 Ap'66 8

Indebtedness among colliery workers. *econ and Political Wkly* 10(31) 2 Ag'75 1147-50

Liberation of coal mine slaves. *Link* 14(4) 14 Nv'71 33-34

COAL mines and mining

Coalmine lessees to be asked to go slow with expansion plans. *TI* 13 Ap'69 1 : 7-8+

COMMERCE

Export potential survey of Bihar. A.C. Vyas *Foreign Trade Rev* 7(1) Ap-Je'72 89-100 tabs

IIFT plan to raise Bihar's annual exports to Rs 830m in 3 years. *TI* 20 Oc'71 4 : 2-3

COMMUNAL riots

Bihar : Now Ranchi. *Link* 16(36) 14 Ap'74 17-19

Muslim polygamy must go if Ranchi-Jamshedpur tribals are not to flare up again. *Organiser* 18(14) 16 Nv'64 9

Rourkela and Jamshedpur : What happened—How and why. *Organiser* 17(42) 18 My'64 5+

See also

Sursand—Communal riots

COMMUNALISM

Against communalism. *Link* 8(13) 7 Nv'65 15

Communalists again active. *Link* 11(16) 1 De'68 16-17

Spurt in communal activity in Bihar. *Link* 14(23) 16 Ja'72 24

COMMUNIST Party (India) : Bihar unit

Bihar C.P.I. calls for consultative bodies to implement programme. *New Age* 15(14) 2 Ap'67 11

Bihar CPI conference. K. Gopalan *New Age* 12(50) 13 De'64 5 ills

Bihar C.P.I. Council expresses concern over rising prices. *New Age* 15(18) 30 Ap'67 6+

Bihar CPI Council reviews election results. K. Gopalan *New Age* 17(14) 6 Ap'69 12+

Bihar CPI joins ministry to thwart Congress come-back. K. Gopalan *New Age* 16(19) 12 My'68 16

Bihar CPI meet. *Link* 17(23) 19 Ja'75 15-16

Bihar CPI on efforts to forge United Front. *New Age* 16(45) 10 Nv'68 5

Bihar CPI plan for "National campaign". *New Age* 20(24) 11 Je'72 4-5

Bihar CPI plans mass campaign. K. Gopalan *New Age* 19(17) 25 Ap'71 7

Bihar CPI suggests priority items for implementation. *New Age* 20(13) 26 Mr'72 2

Bihar CPI supports post-emergency steps. P.S. Madan *New Age* 23(31) 3 Ag'75 12

Bihar CPI vote goes up by 60 percent. K. Gopalan *New Age* 17(8) 23 Fe'69 4

Bihar CPI warns against Congress-R machinations. K. Gopalan *New Age* 19(29) 18 Jl'71 16

Bihar CPI wins prestige seats. *New Age* 17(7) 16 Fe'69 8-9+; 17(8) 23 Fe'69 10+

Bihar Communist Party will register the big advance. Sadhan Mukherjee *New Age* 17(6) 9 Fe'69 4+

Bihar contigent carries with it unforgetable memory of great march. *New Age* 11(38) 22 Se'63 6

Bihar people await non-Congress govt.; statement by Bihar State Council of CPI. *New Age* 15(10) 5 Mr'67 11

Bihar prepares for party Congress. K. Gopalan *New Age* 16(3) 21 Ja'68 5+

Bihar proposals to raise resources. *New Age* 11(50) 15 De'63 7

CPI candidates for Bihar pool. *New Age* 17(2) 12 Ja'69 6

CPI clarifies attitude towards Paswan Ministry.   *New Age*
19(24)   13 Je'71   12

CPI outlines conditions to rejoin Bihar PVD.   *New Age*
19(45)   7 Nv'71   1

CPI outlines election strategy in Bihar.   *New Age*   20(5)
30 Ja'72   2

CPI regrets triple alliance stance, calls for all-Left unity.
New Age   16(49)   8 De'68   5

CPI threat to Bihar coalition.   *TI*   22 Mr'70   5 : 3-4

CPI to move lowering of ceiling.   *New Age*   19(21)
23 My'71   13

CPI's big growth in strength and influence in Bihar.
K. Gopalan   *New Age*   16(44)   3 Nv'68   4

Communists arrested on forged warrant.   *New Age*   11(9)
3 Mr'63   3

Land reforms only solution, says CPI.   *New Age*   23(24)
15 Je'75   3

Left must unite to fight Right reaction.   *New Age*   10(15)
15 Ap'62   5

National Council resolutions on drought conditions in
Bihar, U.P. and M.P.   *New Age*   14(49)   4 De'66   5

One expelled, six suspended : Bihar takes strong steps. *New
Age*   12(21)   24 Ap'64   3

Party firmly united in Bihar : Assessment of district con-
ferences. K. Gopalan   *New Age*   12(48)   1 Nv'64   20

COMMUNIST Party (Marxist, India) : Bihar unit

Bihar : Unjustified claims of CP(M). K. Gopalan   *New Age*
14(52)   25 De'66   8-9

CPI(M) initiative for a Left and democratic front in Bihar.
People's Democracy   4(11)   17 Mr'68   4

COMMUNITY development

B.D.O. in C.D. set up : Bihar's experience. K.K. Prasad
Kurukshetra   15(7)   Ap'67   10-11

Community development in Chota Nagpur. Jyoti Sen.
Asiatic Soc.   1968,   vii, 100p.   Rs 16   Review
Man in India   51(1)   Ja-Mr'71   80

Community development.   *Kurukshetra*   12(1)   2 Oc'63
63-64

Face to face. Jayaprakash Narayan   *Voluntary Action*   8(1-2)
Ja-Ap'71   3-11

Innovation, response and development in Banari. D.P. Sinha *Man in India* 48(3) Jl-Se'68 225-43 tab bibliogr

The Musahri project. Ranjit Gupta *Voluntary Action* 14(4-5) Jl-Oc'72 3-19 tabs

CONSTANTINE, R.

Famine effectively tamed. *Yojana* 11(11) 11 Je'67 19-21

COOPERATION

Cooperation. *Kurukshetra* 13(1) 2 Oc'64 58-59

Progress in the co-operative sector. *Bihar Inform* 18(13) 16 Jl'70 11+

The tribal co-operatives. *mod Rev* 112(6) De'62 479-81

COOPERATIVE societies

Consumer's co-operative stores. *Bihar Inform* 16(16) 16 Se'68 10+

Progress of co-operative movement in Bihar. *Bihar Inform* 18(2) 26 Ja'70 39-42

CORRUPTION

Bihar : Firing blank shells. *Link* 16(10) 14 Oc'73 22-23

Bureaucrats plot sabotage of Aiyar Commission work. K. Gopalan *New Age* 16(37) 15 Se'68 4

A clear case for inquiry; editorial. *TI* 28 Ag'73 4 : 1-2

Corrupt bureaucracy. *Link* 11(5) 15 Se'68 16-18

. How the Mishra family looted Kosi Project. Ravindra Kishore *Organiser* 27(5) 8 Se'73 5

192 charges : Six former Congress ministers in Bihar in the dock. *New Age* 16(4) 28 Ja'68 8-9

River of scandal. N.K. Singh *econ and Political Wkly* 8(37) 15 Se'73 1673-74

The sordid story of the sins of Bihar Congress ministers. *Organiser* 21(26) 4 Fe'68 15

Sri C.R. Pant rules Bihar. Girish Mishra and Braj Kumar Pandey *Mainstream* 7(41) 14 Je'69 24-27

CORRUPTION (in politics)

After the verdict; editorial. *TI* 10 Fe'70 6 : 1

Aiyar panel report. *Link* 12(27) 15 Fe'70 14-15

Fair verdict; editorial. *TI* 13 De'69 6 : 1-2

Housing swindle. *Link* 9(38) 30 Ap'67 14

How corrupt is K.B.? 400 page memo against Bihar Chief Minister submitted to President. *Organiser* 18(21) 4 Ja'65 1-2

Mudolkar body for debarring defector ministers from poll. *TI* 12 De'69 1 : 7-8+

Ramgarh Raja indicted. *Link* 12(19) 21 De'69 15-16

Sahay, 5 others held guilty of power misuse. *TI* 8 Fe'70 1 : 1-2+

Shady deals. *Link* 9(42) 28 My'67 21-22

Six guilty men of Bihar; Aiyar Commission findings. C.N. Ranjan *Organiser* 23(28) 21 Fe'70 4+

Sri C.R. Pant rules Bihar : Girish Mishra and Braj Kumar Pandey *Mainstream* 7(41) 14 Je'69 24-27

COST and standard of living

Levels of living in rural areas in Bihar. C.P. Shastri *Indian J agric Econ* 18(1) Ja-Mr'63 302-10 tabs

Levels of living in rural house-holds. Satish Chandra Jha *Indian J agric Econ* 18(1) Ja-Mr'63 311-16 tabs

COTTAGE industries

Cottage industries of tribal Chota Nagpur. P.C. Roy Choudhury *Khadi Gramodyog* 13(6) Mr'67 462-64

COTTON powerloom industry and trade

Powerloom : As a vital base for rural industrialisation. K.R.P. Sinha *Bihar Inform* 18(2) 26 Ja'70 29-30

COUNCIL of Ministers

BKD chief expels four defectors : Bihar ministry list soon. *TI* 3 Mr'69 1 : 4-5

Big reshuffle of Bihar portfolios. *TI* 1 My'74 1 : 1

Bihar C.M. directed to exclude Ramgarh from Cabinet. *TI* 14 Mr'69 1 : 1-5

Bihar C.M. to submit list today. *TI* 4 Mr'69 1 : 4+

Bihar cabinet axing may spark crisis. *TI* 19 Ap'74 1 : 1-3

Bihar Chief Minister allots portfolios. *TI* 2 Mr'70 1 : 4-5

Bihar controversy still unresolved. *TI* 23 Ap'74 1 : 1-3

Bihar Governor asks Congress leader to form Ministry. *TI* 22 Fe'69 1 : 7-8+

Bihar ministry revamping faces heavy weather. *TI* 15 Ap'74 1 : 7-8+

Bihar SVD adds six Ministers. *TI* 6 Ap'71 1 : 7

Cabinet expansion in Bihar raises storm. *TI* 23 Fe'70 1 : 4

Cabinet expansion. *Link* 13(5) 13 Se'70 15

Congress rift delays Bihar Cabinet list. *TI* 5 Mr'69 1 : 1-2

Daroga Rai expands ministry : 20 new members sworn in. *TI* 28 Fe'70 11 : 1-2

Dissident leader stays out : Bihar coalition ministry is sworn in. *TI* 8 Mr'69 1 : 1-3

8-man Bihar cabinet sworn in. *TI* 20 Mr'72 5 : 2-3

18 more join Bihar ministry : Total strength swells to 33. *TI* 19 Mr'69 1 : 7-8

Farce in Patna; editorial. *TI* 31 My'73 6 : 1

Farcical; editorial. *TI* 21 Mr'69 8 : 1

15-member Bihar cabinet has five new entrants. *TI* 3 Jl'73 7-8+

Ghafoor holds the baby in Bihar. *Link* 15(48) 8 Jl'73 20

A hesitant new start; editorial. *TI* 19 Ap'74 4 : 1

Implications of Mandal drama. H.M. Jain *Mainstream* 6(26) 24 Fe'68 13-14

Jagjivan Ram's son not to join cabinet. *TI* 25 Ap'74 1 : 7-8+

L.N. Mishra rides again. *Commerce* 127(3244) 7 Jl'73 11-13

Major reshuffle of Bihar cabinet : Seven dropped; 10 inducted. *TI* 28 My'73 1 : 1-3

Mishra holds seven key departments. *TI* 12 Ap'75 1 : 4-5+

More rebels to join Bihar cabinet. *TI* 24 Ap'74 1 : 1-3

New cabinets. *Eastern Econ* 48(12) 24 Mr'67 543-44+

New Ministers in Bihar sworn in. *TI* 7 Se'71 1 : 8+

New SVD ministry in Bihar. K. Gopalan *New Age* 16(13) 31 Mr'68 16

No early expansion of Bihar cabinet. *TI* 24 Ap'74 1 : 7-8+

No hasty expansion of Bihar cabinet. *TI* 27 Fe'70 1 : 3

Paswan ministry is expanded. *TI* 25 Je'69 1 : 5-6+

A pattern in power distribution : Bihar. *Commerce* 124(3178) 1 Ap'72 779-80

Persons and pressures. *Link* 6(9) 13 Oc'63 15-16

Portfolios reallocated in Bihar. *TI* 22 Se'71 7 : 2

Problem state; editorial. *TI* 9 Se'71 6 : 1

Problems for new chief. *Link* 11(31) 16 Mr'69 17-18

Ramgarh quits govt; assails central Congress leadership. *TI* 29 Mr'69 1 : 7-8+

Rumblings over composition of ministry. *TI* 3 Jl'73 1 : 6-8+

Scandalous; editorial. *TI* 13 Fe'71 6 : 1

Shady deals. *Link* 9(42) 28 My'67 21-22

Swearing-in of Bihar cabinet today : Raja of Ramgarh included. *TI* 7 Mr'69 1 : 6-7+

23 new Bihar Ministers take oath, 14 absent. *TI* 29 My'73 1 : 1-2

24 Bihar Ministers resign : Hectic activity by revels. *TI* 23 Je'73 1 : 7-8+

35 Bihar Ministers dropped. *TI* 19 Ap'74 1 : 3+

Two claimants for a ministry in Bihar. *TI* 25 Fe'69 1 : 1-2

COUTO, A.F.

Opportunities for industrial growth. *Commerce (Suppl)* 127(3263) 17 Nv'73 31-39

CRANIOLOGY

Anatomical description of two crania from Ramgarh : An ancient site in Dhalbhum, Bihar. Kenneth A.R. Kennedy *J Indian anthrop Soc* 7(2) Oc'72 129-41 tabs figs bibliogr

DA COSTA, E.P.W.

Bihar can save Cong(R) from coalition. *TI* 24 Ja'71 1 : 2-4+

A gallup report on the mid-term elections : Bihar : The confusion of tongues. *Monthly Comm on Indian econ Conditions (Suppl)* 10(6) Ja'69 xi-xiii; *TI* 30 Ja'69 1 : 3-5+; 31 Ja'69 1 : 2-4+

DAMODAR Valley Corporation

The D.V.C. and Bihar. Karuna K. Nandi *mod Rev* 113(3) Mr'63 182-83

DANDAVATE, Madhu

The voice of silence. *Janata* 29(28) 15 Ag'74 23-25

DAS, Amal Kumar and others

Material and socio-religious life of some communities in Purnea. *Bull Cult Res Inst* 3(3-4) 1964 1-15 tabs

DAS, Arvind Narayan

A flood of doubt and hope. *econ and Political Wkly* 9(37) 14 Se'74 1564-65

Murder to landlords' order. *econ and Political Wkly* 10(24) 14 Je'75 915-17

Revolt in slow motion. *econ and Political Wkly* 9(50) 14 De'74 2049-51

DAS, B.L.

Findings of 1971 census in Bihar. *Commerce (Suppl)* 127(3263) 17 Nv'73 45-49 tabs

DAS, B.N.

See Ambastha, C.K. jt. auth.

DAS, J.S.

Small industries in Bihar : Immense scope for growth. *Bihar Inform* 16(12) 1 Jl'68 3-5

DAS, K.K. Lal

Trends of urbanisation in Central Mithila. *Mainstream* 11(45) 7 Jl'73 21-24 tabs

DAS, Naren

Bihar—The path finder. *Janata* 29(39) 10 Nv'74 3-4

DAS, Sunil

The tocsin tolls. *Janata* 29(23) 14 Jl'74 11-12

DASGUPTA, Ajoy

B.P.T.U.C. Special Convention : Pleads to increase production. *New Age* 11(1) 6 Ja'63 15

DASGUPTA, Prabhat

Bihar's rural poor in bitter confrontation with landlords. *New Age* 22(44) 3 Nv'74 3+

Flood and drought, JP and Gafoor too. *New Age* 22(38) 22 Se'74 16+

12 million people face starvation in South Bihar. *New Age* 22(39) 29 Se'74 8 9

DATTA, A.B.

"Democracy in action in the villages of Bihar, Orissa and West Bengal." *quart J Local Self-Government Inst* 36(1) Jl-Se'65 97-103

DATTA, K.K.

Bihar affairs in 1756-58. *J Indian Hist* 40(3) De'62 781-801

Governors and Deputy-Governors of Bihar in the eighteenth century. *Bengal Past & Present* 81(1) Ja-Je'62 32-36 ft-n

A note on historical records and state central archives in Bihar. *Indian Arch* 15 Ja'63-De'64 1-7

DE, Balaram

A comparative study on taste-blindness among the caste group of West Bengal and Munda and Oraon of Ranchi, Bihar. *Bull Cult Res Inst* 9(1-2) 1972 82-83 tabs bibliogr

DESAI, D.K. and Hari Prakash

Planning and implementation of financing agriculture through area approach. (A case study in Bihar State). IIM. 1973, 148p. Rs 7 Review
Indian J agric Econ 28(3) Jl-Se'73 83-86

Planning and implementation of financing the area development scheme. *econ and Political Wkly (Suppl)* 7(31) 25 Mr'72 A13-A22

DESAI, Z.A.

The Indo-Islamic architecture of Bihar. *Islamic Cult* 46(1) Ja'72 17-38

DEV, S. Kumar

President's rule for Bihar? *Commerce* 126(3243) 30 Je'73 1282

DEV DUTT

Bihar : The great defreeze. *Gandhi Marg* 19(1) Ja'75 92-101

DEVELOPMENT administration

Co-ordination of development programmes at the district level with special reference to the role of the district officer in Bihar. Haridwar Rai *Indian J Publ Adm* 12(1) Ja-Mr'66 28-59 bibliogr-ft-n

DHADDA, Siddharaj

See Gangrade, K.D. jt. auth.

DHANESHWAR, Amarendra

Janata Sarkar at Raghopur—A revolution in the making. *Janata* 30(14) 1975 15-16

DHARMARAJAN, S.

Patna after the deluge—A trail of misery and destruction. *TI* 22 Se'75 4 : 3-5; 23 Se'75 4 : 7-8

DIGHWARA

Dighwara : A urban 'service centre' in the lower Ghaghara-Gandak Doab. Rama Shanker Lal *nat Geographical J India* 14(2-3) Je-Se'69 200-13 tabs maps bibliogr-ft-n

DINESHWAR PRASAD

Economic aspects of fisheries development in Bihar. *Indian J agric Econ* 23(4) Oc-De'68 239-42

DISTRICT administration

Economics of new districts. *Commerce* 119(3058) 13 De'69 1132

DISTRICTS

District profile : General : 1971. *Commerce (Suppl)* 127(3263) 17 Nv'73 90

DRAINAGE

Geomorphological evolution of stream order of the Topa and Silphi basins in Ranchi. R.P. Singh and A. Kumar *nat Geographical J India* 15(1) Mr'69 38-44 tabs figs

DROUGHTS

The drought in Bihar and U.P.; editorial. Sadiq Ali *AICC econ Rev* 18(10) 1 De'66 3-4

Grave drought situation in Bihar. *TI* 28 Se'72 1 : 1-4+

In drought-stricken Bihar. Deoki Nandan Singh *ill Wkly India* 87(52) 25 De'66 24-25

DUTT, Ashok Kumar

Physical basis of the city of Jamshedpur—An urban study. *Deccan Geographer* 3(1) Ja'65 1-10 bibliogr

DUTT, J.

Motipur : A village outstanding. *Kurukshetra* 14(11) Ag'66 14-16 tabs

DUTTA, S.K.

Prolonged neglect of Cachar leads to political discontent. *TI* 23 My'75 4 : 7-8

ECONOMIC conditions

Bihar C.P.I. Council expresses concern over rising prices. *New Age* 15(18) 30 Ap'67 6+

Bihar continuing battle. Jagannath Sarkar *New Age* 21(14) 8 Ap'73 6

Bihar disturbances. *Link* 8(3) 29 Ag'65 17

Bihar's abysmal poverty : Millions in bondage. Janak Singh *TI* 23 Se'74 4 : 7-8

A confusing picture. Chandra Mohan Mishra *Link* 16(25) 26 Ja'74 37-38

Economic condition of North Bihar. Subhash Chandra Sarkar *mod Rev* 124(2) Fe'69 121-28; 124(3) Mr'69 183-89 tabs

The economics of a backward region in a backward economy : A case study of Bihar in relation to other states of India. Kedarnath Prasad. Scientific bk Ag. 2 Vols. xvi, 584p. Rs 45 Review
AICC econ Rev 20(19) 15 Ap'69 33; *Commerce* 118(3030) 31 My'69 10 8; *Eastern Econ* 52(4) 24 Ja'69 142-43; *Link* 11(31) 16 Mr'69 48

Economics of Bihar politics. Subhash Chandra Sarkar *mod Rev* 124(4) Ap'70 262-67 bibliogr-ft-n

*Economy of Bihar. S.R. Bose. Mukhopadhyay

Famine under control; an interview. Mahamaya Prasad Sinha *Yojana* 11(9) 14 My'67 2-4+

Flood and drought. *Link* 7(51) 1 Ag'65 18

Four crore people of the Bihar on brink of starvation. Balbir Dutt *Organiser* 27(38) 27 Ap'74 13

'*Garibi hatao andolan*' in Bihar. Parimal Mukherjee *Yojana* 17(5) 1 Ap'73 225-27

Hundred years after; editorial *econ and Political Wkly* 7(19) 6 My'72 907

Impact of the struggle for freedom on the socio-economic structure in Bihar. *Bihar Inform* 18(4) 15 Ag'70 56-59

The internal colony. Sachchidanand Sinha. Sindhu Pub. 1973, vi, 159p. Rs 25 Review
Sociological Bull 23(1) Mr'74 144-47

Light versus darkness. S.M. Joshi *Janata* 29(28) 15 Ag'74 **5-8**

Monograph of Bihar : A geographical study. R.P. Singh and Anil Kumar. Bharati Bhawan. 1970, 193p. Review *nat Geographical J India* 17(4) De'71 **215**

Pilgrimage to Patna. Hartiruth Singh *AICC econ Rev* 13(17) 22 Ja'62 8-10

Poverty amidst plenty. *Thought* 28(40) 5 Oc'68 10

Production relations : Achilles' heel of Indian planning. Pradhan H. Prasad *econ and Political Wkly* 8(19) 12 My'73 869-72

Prolonged neglect of Cachar leads to political discontent. S.K. Dutta *TI* 23 My'75 4 : 7-8

A question of courage. *Link* 5(28) 17 Fe'63 13-14

Richest resources, poorest development. Balbir Dutt *Organiser* 25(36) 15 Ap'72 25-26

The semi-proletariat of rural Bihar. Pradhan Prasad   *Call*
26(4)   De'74   8-13   tabs

A spectre is haunting Bihar.   *econ and Political Wkly*   1(16)
3 De'66   655-57

Syndrome of underdevelopment. N.K. Singh   *econ and
Political Wkly*   7(38)   10 Se'72   1909-10

*Techno-economic survey of Bihar. N.C.A.E.R.; Asia. Vol 1.
1959, xvi, 276p. tabs maps bibliogr 25cm. Rs 17.50

Wheat take-over hits the economy.   *Commerce (Suppl)*
127(3250)   18 Ag'73   17-19

A year of crisis.   *Commerce (Suppl)*   129(3301)   17 Ag'74
17-21

   See also
Food supply

ECONOMIC development

Bihar lacks infrastructure. R.J. Venkateswaran   *Eastern
Econ*   59(7)   18 Ag'72   412-14   tabs

Bihar on the march.   *Indian Fin*   91(13)   6 Ap'73   325-26

Bihar records all-rounds progress. Surendra Sen Mehta
Yojana   17(9)   1 Je'73   379-80

Bihar's tardy economic growth : Diagnosis and prescription. Kedarnath Prasad   *Southern Econ*   12(21)   1 Mr'74
19-22

Economic characteristics of Musahri block area—Part 1.
Voluntary Action   13(6)   Nv-De'71   24-28   tabs

The economy of Bihar.   *Commerce (Suppl)*   127(3263)
17 Nv'73   12-22   tabs figs

Infrastructure for stat-s-3 : Bihar : Accent on irrigation.
Commerce (Annual Num ber)   119(3061)   1969   139

A novel experiment in Bihar. Sachchidanand   *Commerce
(Suppl)*   127(3263)   17 Nv'73   69-73

Perspective of power development in Bihar. B.N. Sahu
AICC econ Rev   18(17)   15 Mr'67   37-39

Socio-cultural implications of economic development in
Banari : The case of Birhor resettlement. D.P. Sinha
Eastern Anthropologist   20(2)   My-Ag'67   109-32   bibliogr-ft-n

Strains on state finances.   *Commerce (Suppl)*   131(3352)
16 Ag'75   15-17

Whither Bihar; editorial.   *Eastern Econ*   53(5)   1 Ag'69
191-92

See also

River-valley projects

_____ : Statistics

Bihar in India's economy. *Commerce (Suppl)* 127(3263)
17 Nv'73 87-88

ECONOMIC history

Changing agrarian economy of Purnea district : 1765-1950.
Madaneshwar Mishra *J Bihar Res Soc* 58(1-4) Ja-De'72
197-223 tabs bibliogr-ft-n

Indigo plantation and the agrarian relations in Champaran
during the nineteenth century. Girish Mishra *Indian econ
soc Hist Rev* 3(4) De'66 332-57 bibliogr

Socio-economic background of Gandhi's Champaran Movement. Girish Mishra *Indian econ soc Hist Rev* 5(3) Se'68
245-75 tabs bibliogr-ft-n

*Socio-religious, economic and literary condition of Bihar
from 319 A.D. to 1000 A.D.). Bhagvatisaran Varma.
Munshiram. 1962, xii, 209p. 36 pls bibliogr 24.5cm.
Rs 24

See also

Land tenure : History

Mines and mineral resources : History

ECONOMIC planning

Annual plan of Rs 180 crores. *Commerce* 130(3324)
1 Fe'75 105-07

*Bihar through two plans. Bihar, Public Relations Dept.
1961, ii, 45p.

Bihar's fifth plan : An appraisal. D.N. Jha *Southern Econ*
13(4) 15 Je'74 19-21

Bihar's fourth five-year plan. *Eastern Econ* 42(26) 26 Je'64
1458-59

*Bihar's third plan at a glance. Bihar, Publ Relations
Dept. 1961, ii, 45p.

Emergency plan. *Link* 8(12) 31 Oc'65 18-19

An integrated development planning for a backward area
of a backward district in Bihar. S.P. Sinha and B.N. Verma
Indian J agric Econ 28(4) Oc-De'73 53-54

Marginal increase in real investment. *Commerce* 127(3259)
20 Oc'73 701-02

Outlay under state plans. *Commerce (Suppl)* 127(3263)
17 Nv'73 90

Planning and agricultural development. D N. Jha.
S. Chand. 1974, 232p. Rs 30 Review
Indian J industr Relations 10(4) Ap'75 615-17

Planning at the state and district levels. K N. Tiwary
J nat Acad Adm 15(4) Oc-De'70 145-54 bibliogr-ft-n

Rs 1,267-crore fifth plan for Bihar. *Commerce* 128(3276)
23 Fe'74 207-09

Sheaving the plan. *Link* 5(22) 6 Ja'63 17

Towards an approach to the fifth plan for Bihar. Pradhan
H. Prasad *Mankind* 16(1) Ag-Oc'72 27-33

Twice the third plan. *Link* 8(1) 15 Ag'65 51

ECONOMIC policy

Bihar : An uphill task. Abdul Ghafoor *Link* 16(25)
26 Ja'74 35-37

Bihar coalition adopts 33-point programme; text of programme adopted by the parties in the coalition government.
Organiser 20(31) 19 Mr'67 7

Bihar government takes some progressive steps; but land-
lord pressure continues. K. Gopalan *New Age* 20(27)
2 Jl'72 13

Bihar Governor outlines Front's programme, policies.
K. Gopalan *New Age* 15(13) 26 Mr'67 6

Bihar : Mishra starts with big goodwill. P.S. Madan *New
Age* 23(20) 18 My'75 11

Bihar shall not suffer; editorial. *New Age* 20(39) 24 Se'72 2

Bihar's first non-Congress ministry. *Link* 9(31) 12 Mr'67
12-14

Implementation of 20-point programme : Powerhouse cob-
webs swept off in Bihar. *New Age* 23(31) 3 Ag'75 13

Non-Congress ministry takes office in Bihar. *New Age*
15(11) 12 Mr'67 5

Pampering the affluent farmers. *Commerce* 120(3069)
28 Fe'70 381

Programme of the non-Congress government (Documents).
United Asia 19(2) Mr-Ap'67 133-35

A temporary expedient; editorial. *TI* 3 Jl'73 6 : 1-2

EDUCATION

Cleaning it up; editorial. *TI* 3 Jl'72 6 : 1-2

The role of education in modernization of Chotanagpur.
L.R.N. Srivastava *Indian educ Rev* 6(1) Ja'71 162-82 bibliogr

Thorough probe. *Link* 6(48)   12 Jl'64   40-41

EDUCATION and state

Gulf of commissions. *Link* 8(48)   10 Jl'66   12-13

ELECTIONS

And now the lesson of Banka; editorial. *Thought*   25(17)
28 Ap'73   3-4

Another spell of political instability. *Commerce* 118(3016)
22 Fe'69   313-14

Arrah firing may affect adversely Congress prospects.   *TI*
18 Ja'69   5 : 5-8

BJS performance in Bihar poll. Thakur Prasad   *Organiser*
22(28)   22 Fe'69   16+

Banka rout due to PCC rift.   *TI*   21 Ap'73   1 : 6-8+

Bihar : Blasted Swatantra hopes. *Link*   4(26)   4 Fe'62
17-18

Bihar CPI council reviews elections results.   K. Gopalan
New Age 17(14)   6 Ap'69   12+

Bihar : CPI holds its own fighting all alone.   K. Gopalan
New Age   19(12)   21 Mr'71   7

Bihar-CPI vote goes up by 60 percent. K. Gopalan   *New
Age*   17(8)   23 Fe'69   4

Bihar-CPI wins prestige seats   *New Age*   17(7)   16 Fe'69
8-9+

Bihar : CPM aligns with Syndicate—Jana Sangh. K. Gopalan   *New Age*   20(9)   27 Fe'72   8

Bihar can save Cong(R) from coalition. E.P.W. Da Costa
TI   24 Ja'71   1 : 2-4+

Bihar : Caste factor. *Link*   9(25)   26 Ja'67   34+

Bihar Communist Party will register big advance. Sadhan
Mukherjee *New Age*   17(6)   9 Fe'69   4+

Bihar-Communists double seats. Ali Ashraf   *New Age*
10(10)   11 Mr'62   2

Bihar : Confidence grows. *Link*   14(29)   27 Fe'72   18-19

Bihar : Confusing picture. *Link*   11(27)   16 Fe'69   12

Bihar Congress backs out from commitments. K. Gopalan
New Age   19(7)   14 Fe'71   8-9

Bihar Congress bid to reduce elections to farce. K. Gopalan
New Age   15(7)   12 Fe'67   6

Bihar Congress in good shape : Opposition in disarray. Jitendra Singh *TI* 8 Fe'69 6 : 7-8

Bihar Congress on the run. *Organiser* 20(25) 29 Ja'67 5+

Bihar Congress resorts to pressure tactics. K. Gopalan *New Age* 19(6) 7 Fe'71 7

Bihar Congress to have adjustment with CPI and PSP. *TI* 5 Fe'72 1 : 7-8

Bihar : Dim hopes of stability. *Link* 11(26) 9 Fe'69 14+

Bihar efforts to forge left united front. K. Gopalan *New Age* 16(38) 22 Se'68 7

Bihar : Election expenses in the midst of famine.   *Capital* 158(3946) 2 Fe'67 217

Bihar election scene : Struggle for left democratic front. Indradeep Sinha *New Age* 16(50) 15 De'68 5+

Bihar : Ghafoor victory. *Link* 16(30) 3 Mr'74 9-10

Bihar in the cesspool of instability. Girish Mishra and Braj Kumar Pandey *Mainstream* 7(30) 29 Mr'69 11-12+

Bihar key contest : Karpoori Thakur may retain seat. *TI* 27 Fe'72 5 : 3-4

Bihar mosaic. Girish Mishra *Mainstream* 9(25) 20 Fe'71 11+

Bihar people await non-Congress popular govt; statement by Bihar State Council of CPI. *New Age* 15(10) 5 Mr'67 11

Bihar poll results—An analysis. K. Gopalan *New Age* 20(14) 2 Ap'72 8

Bihar poll results. *mod Rev* 124(3) Mr'69 209

Bihar : Reaction fails to forge united front. K. Gopalan *New Age* 20(8) 20 Fe'72 11

Bihar : Stability eludes the state. *Janata* 24(6)   2 Mr'69 9-10

Bihar steps to ensure smooth poll. *TI* 19 Ja'69   15 : 1

Bihar : Unjustified claims of CP(M). K. Gopalan *New Age* 14(52) 25 De'66 8-9

Bright chances for Congress in Muzaffarpur. *TI* 24 Ja'69 5 : 1

By-election impact. *Link* 7(18) 13 De'64 16-19

By-election in a Bihar Assembly Constituency : Study in voting behaviour. Nagesh Jha *econ and Political Wkly* 1(10) 22 Oc'66 417-20 tabs

CPI candidates for Bihar poll. *New Age* 17(2) 12 Ja'69 6

CPI Kedar's will win Jamshedpur seat. Sadhan Mukherjee *New Age* 19(10) 7 Mr'71 12

CPI main contender in Buxar against Ram Subhag Singh. Sudarshan Bhatia *TI* 19 Fe'71 5 : 1-2

CPI outlines election strategy in Bihar. *New Age* 20(5) 30 Ja'72 2

CPI regrets triple alliance stance, calls for all-left unity. *New Age* 16(49) 8 De'68 5

CPI-35, Congress-167, PSP-4 : Big victory of Bihar electoral entente. Sadhan Mukherjee *New Age* 20(12) 19 Mr'72 7

CPI welcomes midterm election in Bihar. K. Gopalan *New Age* 20(1) 2 Ja'72 11

Caste equations, new factors. *Link* 13(27) 14 Fe'71 20-22

Casting on caste sentiment. *Thought* 23(7) 23 Fe'71 10

Challenge and opportunity. Girish Mishra *Mainstream* 10(30) 25 Mr'72 10-12

Changing colours of Congress-R candidate. Sadhan Mukherjee *New Age* 19(8) 21 Fe'71 4

Christian and Muslim role in Bihar poll. Balbir Dutt *Organiser* 22(29) 1 Mr'69 6+

Communist influence on the wane in Champaran district. *TI* 4 Fe'69 7 : 1-3

Cong needs 25 more for majority in Bihar. *TI* 14 Mr'72 9 : 3-4

Cong(R) sure to farewell in Bihar. Jitendra Singh *TI* 15 Ja'71 1 : 7-8+

Congress, CPI and PSP unity in Bihar vindicated. *Link* 14(32) 19 Mr'72 18-19

Congress has clear edge over others in Muzaffarpur. *TI* 6 Fe'69 5 : 7-8

Congress has increased its vote in Bihar. *TI* 18 Mr'72 11 : 5

Congress hopes and fears. *econ and Political Wkly* 7(3) 15 Ja'72 102-03

Congress may secure 50 p.c. seats in Darbhanga. *TI* 5 Fe'69 5 : 6-8

Congress on road to victory in Bihar. *TI* 13 Mr'72 7 : 1

Congress to probe Banka poll debacle. *TI* 20 Ap'73 1 : 8+

Congress victory in Orissa, Bihar uncertain. *Eastern Econ* 48(6) 10 Fe'67 240-41

Congressmen to defeat party nominees in Gaya. *TI* 29 Ja'69 5 : 5-6

Darbhanga by-election result shows reactionaries still strong in Bihar. *New Age* 20(6) 6 Fe'72 1

Defeating Congress, Jana Sangh : CPI wins Ramgarh by big margin. *New Age* 20(21) 21 My'72 7

Devious ways of reactionary combine. Girish Mishra *Mainstream* 10(27) 4 Mr'72 9-10+

Election panorama in Bihar. Chetkar Jha *Political Sci Rev* 6(3-4)-7(1-2) Jl-Se'67-Ap-Je'68 139-51 tabs

Election preview-VII : Bihar may have another spell of instability. *TI* 22 Fe'72 1 : 1-5+

Election results at a glance-4. *Yojana* 11(9) 14 My'67 16

Election scene in Chotanagpur. *New Age* 19(4) 24 Ja'71 7

Elections prospects in U.P. and Bihar. *Organiser* 22(21) 4 Ja'69 14-15

End of Congress bungling? *Link* 13(28) 21 Fe'71 17-20

Exciting battle. *Link* 11(25) 2 Fe'69 11-13

Four straight contests in Bihar elections. *TI* 14 Fe'72 5 : 2-3

From the ballot box. *Eastern Econ* 48(12) 24 Mr'67 519+

Front bid to defeat Jagjivan Ram. Sudarshan Bhatia *TI* 19 Fe'71 7 : 1-2

Further list of Bihar candidates. *TI* 11 Fe'70 5 : 1-3

A gallup report on the mid-term elections : Bihar : The confusion of tongues. E.P.W. da Costa *Monthly Comm on Indian econ Conditions (Suppl)* 10(6) Ja'69 xi-xiii; *TI* 30 Ja'69 1 : 3-5+; 31 Ja'69 1 : 2-4+

Mrs Gandhi denounces Jana Sangh and LTD. *TI* 22 Ja'69 5 : 3-4

Giant killer has tough rival in Goreakothi. *TI* 5 Mr'72 5 : 1-3

Hard fight ahead of new Congress in Bihar. Dilip Mukherjee *TI* 28 Fe'71 1 : 2-4+

High hopes for coalition. *Janata* 23(50) 12 Ja'69 13

Hopes for Left in Bihar. *Link* 11(23) 19 Ja'69 14

Instability continues. Girish Mishra and Braj Kumar Pandey *Mainstream* 7(25) 22 Fe'69 9-10+

JS may find it hard to retain seat Monghyr. *TI* 5 Mr'72 5 : 4

Jagjivan Ram's blackmail tactics exposed. *New Age* 19(11) 14 Mr'71 2

Jai Jamshedpur! *New Age* 10(11) 18 Mr'62 3

Jana Sangh bid to emerge largest single party. *Organiser* 25(30) 4 Mr'72 9+

Jana Sangh establishes firm foothold in Bihar. *Organiser* 15(32) 26 Mr'62 4+

Jana Sangh is the second biggest force in Bihar. *Organiser* 24(33) 27 Mr'71 4 tabs

Jana Sangh will emerge as the largest single party in Bihar. *Organiser* 22(24) 26 Ja'69 37-38

Jobless adivasi youth's bid to storm Jharkhand citadel. *TI* 10 Mr'72 11 : 2-3

Karpoori Thakur will contest from Tajpur. *TI* 8 Fe'72 4 : 1-2

Key Bihar by election. *Link* 16(27) 10 Fe'74 14-15

Key by election in Bihar. *Link* 14(22) 9 Ja'72 12-13

Large-scale voting in Bihar. Beni Shankar Sharma *Organiser* 22(31) 15 Mr'69 11+

Left will gain. *Link* 9(27) 12 Fe'67 23 ills

Leftward swing. *Link* 9(29) 26 Fe'67 18-19

List of Congress candidates for Bihar Assembly poll. *TI* 7 Fe'72 4 : 1-3

Losers all. *econ and Political Wkly* 4(9) 1 Mr'69 423-25 tab

M.P. Sinha facing tough contest in Maharajganj. *TI* 31 Ja'69 7 : 3-5

Mid term poll : Factionalism rife. *Link* 11(16) 1 De'68 13-24

Ministers in trouble. *Link* 9(28) 19 Fe'67 16-17

Mishra for review of Congress-CPI relations in Bihar. *TI* 21 Ap'73 1 : 7-8+

Most parties are faced with internal quarrels. Sudarshan Bhatia *TI* 16 Fe'71 5 : 4-5

Multi-cornered contests. *Commerce* 118(3012) 25 Ja'69 118

Multi-cornered contests in many constituencies. *TI* 12 Ja'69 5 : 4-5

Must mistakes be repeated? Anjani K. Sinha *Mainstream* 8(20) 18 Ja'69 11-13

Muzaffarpur bye election : Communists help rout reaction. *New Age* 11(16) 21 Ap'63 15

No party may win absolute majority in Bihar. *TI* 10 Ja'69 5 : 1-3

Odds against Congress. *Link* 9(22) 8 Ja'67 17

PSP list for mid-term poll in Bihar. *TI* 2 Ja'69 3 ; 6

Paswan in for grim fight in Korha. *TI* 3 Mr'72 4 : 1-3

Paswan's colleagues in former cabinet get Congress ticket. *TI* 7 Fe'72 1 : 7-8+

Patna (west) results anybody's guess. *TI* 2 Fe'69 7 : 1-3

Peaceful but cool polling in Bihar. *Link* 14(31) 12 Mr'72 14

Poised for another crushing blow to Congress. Jagannath Sarkar *New Age* 17(5) 2 Fe'69 3

Politics of immobilise—Selecting Congress candidates in Bihar. Ramashray Ray *Political Sci Rev* 6(3-4)-7(1-2) Jl-Se'67-Ap-Je'68 41-58 bibliogr-ft-n

Poll fails to break Bihar stalemate. *TI* 14 Fe'69 1 : 4-5

Poll prospects Chotanagpur : New equations in changed situation. Dipankar Gupta *Mainstream* 9(23) 6 Fe'71 12-13+

Poll tensions. *Link* 8(34) 3 Ap'66 11-12

Prospects for Congress in Bihar are bleak. *Organiser* 15(24) 29 Ja'62 5+

Reaction's all-round retreat. Girish Mishra and Braj Kumar Pandey *Mainstream* 9(30) 27 Mr'71 17-20

Reader's ready reference to Lok Sabha election : Bihar. *Mainstream* 9(25) 20 Fe'71 24-27

Remote chance of stability. *econ and Political Wkly* 4(4) 25 Ja'69 240-41

SSP grip on Monghyr becoming loose. *TI* 1 Fe'69 9 : 3-4

The same old Congress. *econ and Political Wkly* 7(9) 26 Fe'72 498-99

The seven blindmen. N.K. Singh   *econ and Political Wkly*
8(18)   5 Mr'73   824-25

77 candidates in Bihar. *Janata*   23(50)   12 Ja'69   14

She came with a smile but left with a scowl. *Organiser*
22(22)   11 Ja'69   1+

State govt's indifference. *Link*   13(31)   14 Mr'71   14-15

A study of mid-term elections in Bihar 1969. V.P. Verma,
ed. Inst of Public Adm (Univ of Patna). 1971, 318p. Rs 15
Review
Indian Political Sci Rev   6(2)   Ap-Se'73 256-57; *South Asian
Stud*   6(1)   Ja'71   88-90

Tarkeshwari Sinha faces stiff contest. Jitendra Singh   *TI*
6 Mr'72   5 : 4-5

Two Bhimihars main contenders. Jitendra Singh   *TI*
22 Fe'71   5 : 6-7

Unity will help. *Link*   8(1)   15 Ag'65   59

Very little has changed. *econ and Political Wkly* 7(8) 19 Fe'72
452-53

Violence in Bihar on polling day. S.C. Sarker   *ill Wkly
India* 90(9)   2 Mr'69   14

Violence—Main plank of reaction in Bihar. K. Gopalan
New Age   19(11)   14 Mr'71   3

Whipping up caste hysteria. *Link*   13(28)   28 Fe'71 16-19

Wind in Bihar favours left democratic forces. K. Gopalan
New Age   19(9)   28 Fe'71   10

_____ : Statistics

Details of election results from Bihar. *TI*   15 Fe'69 9 : 1-6

ELECTRIC power

Making up the gap in power supply. Jagannath Mishra
Commerce (Suppl)   127(3263)   17 Nv'73   23-24

Patratu debacle; editorial. *econ and Political Wkly*   7(22)
27 My'72   1044-45

Power needs of West Bengal and Bihar during third plan.
Capital   148(3699)   1 Mr'62   365-68

Power supply in W. Bengal and Bihar. *Eastern Econ*   38(9)
2 Mr'62   601-04

The saga of electricity in Bihar. B.N. Ojha   *Commerce
(Suppl)*   127(3263)   17 Nv'73   59-61

Uncertainty in Patratu power extension. *Commerce*
126(3224)   17 Fe'73   319-20

ELECTRIC utilities

Political and electrical power failure in Bihar. *Organiser* 22(48) 12 Jl'69 14

ELECTRIFICATION

Bihar : Big project, big problems. *Yojana* 12(13) 7 Jl'68 39-42 ills

ENGINEER, B.B.

Mineral and mining resources. *ill Wkly India* 89(12) 24 Mr'68 30-33

ENGINEERING workers

> *See also*
Strikes : Engineering workers

ETHNOLOGY

Levels of economic initiative and ethnic groups in Pargana Barabham. Surajit Sinha *Eastern Anthropologist* 16(2) My-Ag'63 65-74

> *See also*
Santals, The

EXCAVATIONS (Archaeology)

Facts about "gap" in history. *Link* 7(4) 6 Se'64 40

*Report on Kumrahar excavations 1951-1955. Anant Sadasiv Altekar and Vijaykant Misra. K.P. Jayaswal Res Inst. Historical research series). Vol 3. 1959, xvi, 142p. Rs 40

Rich neolithic layer found in Bihar. *TI* 16 Je'69 5 : 1-3

EXCISE department

Activities of the excise department during the last three plan periods. *Bihar Inform* 17(5) 16 Mr'69 12-13+

Excise administration in Bihar. *Bihar Inform* 16(21) 16 De'68 11-12

FAIRS

Fairs and festivals. *ill Wkly India* 89(12) 24 Mr'68 42-44

FAMILY planning

Acceptability and awareness of family planning. B.B. Mandal *Voluntary Action* 16(6) Nv-De'74 29-31 bibliogr

Attitudes and practices of graduate school teachers towards family planning. H.S.M.Q. Akhtar and others *J Family Welfare* 19(1) Se'72 57-65 tabs bibliogr

Bihar : Overcoming handicaps. *Mainstream* 8(16) 21 De'68 33-44

Bihar to have more mobile family planning clinics. *Bihar Inform* 16(16) 16 Se'68 2

Family planning in Bihar. V.P. Kashyap *Bihar Inform* 18(7) 16 Ap'70 1-2

Family planning programmes in Bihar. *Indian Architect (Suppl)* 10(12) De'68 7

Inter-block variations in family planning achievements. G.P.L. Srivastava *J Family Welfare* 20(4) Je'74 34-42 tabs bibliogr

A micro study of motivators in Bihar vasectomy camps. P.K. Jain and B.B.L. Sharma *Voluntary Action* 16(6) Nv-De'74 13-14

Opinion and attitude towards family planning among women of primary school teachers Ishwar Prasad and others *Indian J soc Wk* 23(2) Jl'62 179-83 tabs

Personality adjustment and family planning practices : A case study of secondary school teachers. K.K. Verma and Prabha Shukla *J soc Res* 15(2) Se'72 115-19 tab

A santhal view of birth restraints : A case study. Jayanta Sarkar *J Family Welfare* 17(1) Se'70 44-47 tabs

Some aspects of the Bihar mass vasectomy camps. B.L. Mathur and G.P.L. Srivastava *J Family Welfare* 20(3) Mr'74 73-83 tabs bibliogr

Some common information about family planning. Sushma Nand *Bihar Inform* 17(20) 1 De'69 25-31 bibliogr

Vasectomy : Field experience of a district hospital in Bihar. D.N. Saksena *J Family Welfare* 18(2) De'71 9-19 tabs ft-n

FAMINES

Bihar : Election expenses in the midst of famine. *Capital* 158(3946) 2 Fe'67 217

Bihar : Front ministry grapples with grim legacy of Congress misrule, Unni Krishnan *New Age* 15(21) 21 My'67 3+

Bihar's agony : Famine of food and water. *Commerce* 114(2921) 6 My'67 791

Bihar's man-made famine. Ravindra Kishore *Organiser* 27(6) 15 Se'73 9-10

Centre's antipathy forced Bihar to declare famine. K. Gopalan *New Age* 15(18) 30 Ap'67 11

Contre's role in famine; editorial. *Capital* 158(3958) 27 Ap'67 838-39

Economics of famine. *Commerce* 115(2945) 21 Oc'67 944

The face of hunger in Bihar 1-11. Pauly V. Parakal   *New Age* 14(48) 27 Nv'66 8-10;   14(49) 4 De'66 8-9 ills

Famine effectively tamed. R. Constatine *Yojana* 11(11) 11 Je'67 iv (cover)

Famine relief in Bihar. CIRT. 1970, 385p. Rs 15 Review *Interdiscipline* 7(3) Aut'70 310-12; *soc Action* 20(1) Ja-Mr'70 99-101; *soc Welfare* 16(10) Ja'70 inside cover; *Voluntary Action* 11(5-6) Se-De'69 36

Famine under control; interview. Mahamaya Prasad Sinha *Yojana* 11(9) 14 My'67 2-4+

Famine grips Bihar. K. Gopalan   *New Age* 14(45) 6 Nv'66 4

Famine stalks Bihar, government apathy. *New Age* 20(34) 20 Ag'72 6

Food riots, starvation deaths in Bihar : Government remains passive and complacent. K. Gopalan *New Age* 13(28) 11 Jl'65 1+

A free kitchen that feeds 22,000 people. *Yojana* 11(11) 11 Je'67 iv (cover)

Help Bihar call; CPI National Council resolution, Calcutta, April, 1967. *New Age* 15(19) 7 My'67 9

Jaya Prakashji commends selfless service of RSS workers. *Organiser* 20(29) 26 Fe'67 5

Officials hamper Bihar government's massive famine relief operation. K. Gopalan *New Age* 15(22)   28 My'67 8-9

Sahay's deal with US embassy? *New Age* 14(28) 27 Nv'66 1

State of famine. *Link* 9(37) 23 Ap'67 25-26 ills

Thoughts on Bihar. Carding Jane *ill Wkly India* 88(30) 27 Ag'67 16-17

12 million people face starvation in South Bihar. Prabhat Dasgupta *New Age* 22(39) 29 Se'74 8-9

Unquickened conscience; editorial.   *econ and Political Wkly* 2(16) 22 Ap'67 743-44

What you can do for Bihar-and how...... *Organiser* 20(46) 2 Jl'67 10

Will centre discharge its responsibility? Indradeep Sinha *New Age* 15(19) 7 My'67 12 por

FARMERS

Profile of progressive farmer. Mohammed Omair Alam *Kurukshetra* 20(14) 16 Ap'72 14-15

Selective perception and adoption behaviour of adult farmers. N P. Singh and C. Prasad *Indian J Adult Educ* 35(1)
Ja'74 14-16 tabs

Value orientations of farmers regarding rural living and
farming. N.P. Singh and others *Khadi Gramodyog* 18(9)
Je'72 519-27 tabs

FEDERAL and state fiscal relations
  Bihar's urgent needs; an interview. Indradeep Sinha *Link*
  9(35) 9 Ap'67 24-25

FERNANDES, George
  The final round of battle in Bihar. *Janata* 29(33) 29 Se'74
  7+

FERTILIZER industry and trade
  A study of input (fertilizers) supply condition and marketing mechanism in the district of Saharsa, Bihar. S.P. Sinha
  and B N. Verma *Indian J agric Econ* 28(4) Oc-De'73 154-55

FERTILIZERS and manures
  Attitude of tribals and non-tribals of Ranchi towards
  fertilizers. S. Sanjar F. Alam and others *Man in India* 52(4)
  Oc-De'72 328-34 tabs

  Balanced fertilization. *Farmer and Parliament* 7(11) Nv'72
  22+

  Soil fertility and fertilizer problems in Bihar. S.C. Mandal
  and M.P. Sinha *Indian Fmg* 21(1) Ap'71 5-6+

FESTIVALS
  The annual festivals among the Santals. A.C. Sinha
  Vanyajati 18(2) Ap'70 84-98 bibliogr-ft-n

  Fairs and festivals. R.P.N. Sinha *ill Wkly India* 89(12)
  24 Mr'68 42-44 ills

  Impact of Brahminical culture on the tribes of Chotanagpur : IND festival—A case study. Pashupati Prasad
  Mahato *Folklore* 13(11) Nv'72 452-60 bibliogr

FIELD crops
  Crop-combination regions of North Bihar. Bishweshwar
  Mandal *nat Geographical J India* 15(2) Je'69 125-37 figs
  bibliogr-ft-n

  Economics of crop pattern of irrigated farms in North
  Bihar. Divakar Jha *Indian J agric Econ* 18(1) Ja-Mr'63
  168-69 tabs

  Rains not enough, but crop prospects not bad. H.P.
  Sharma *Yojana* 10(15) 7 Ag'66 5-6

FINANCE, Public

Legacy of inefficiency. *Commerce* 115(2950) 25 Nv'67 1247

Politics in raising resources. *Commerce* 118(3014) 8 Fe'69 212-13

FISHERIES

Development of fisheries—A study of the fishermen cooperative societies in the district of Darbhanga, Bihar. S.P. Sinha and M.N. Jha *Indian J agric Econ* 23(4) Oc-De'68 243-47 tabs

Economic aspects of fisheries development in Bihar. Dineshwar Prasad *Indian J agric Econ* 23(4) Oc-De'68 239-42

FISHERIES, Cooperative

Development of fisheries—A study of the fishermen cooperative societies in the district of Darbhanga, Bihar. S.P. Sinha and M.N. Jha *Indian J agric Econ* 23(4) Oc-De'68 243-47 tabs

FLOODS

Bihar : Dreadful floods. *Link* 13(51) 1 Ag'71 19

Bihar orders probe into causes of floods breaches. *TI* 6 Ag'75 1 : 4-5+

Chavan staggered by magnitude of flood havoc in Bihar. *TI* 19 Ag'71 7 : 1-2

Copters engaged in flood relief. *TI* 8 Ag'75 1 : 1-3+

Cost of bad planning. *Commerce* 115(2943) 7 Oc'67 806-07

Damages by rains and floods in U.P. and Bihar : K.L. Rao's statement in Lok Sabha. *Bihar Inform* 17(16) 16 Se'69 19-20

Flood and drought, JP and Gafoor too. Prabhat Dasgupta *New Age* 22(38) 22 Se'74 16+

Flood in Bihar (1969). *Bihar Inform* 17(16) 16 Se'69 16-18

A flood of memories. A.P. Mote *TI* 28 Se'75 9 : 1-4

Flood situation in Bihar. K.L. Rao *Bihar Inform* 17(15) 1 Se'69 15

Flood situation in North Bihar worsens. *TI* 29 Jl'75 1 : 5-6+

Flood threat to Patna increases. *TI* 26 Jl'71 7 : 2-3

Flood uproots lakhs. *Link* 14(2) 22 Ag'71 16-17

Flood waters enter Monghyr from 3 sides. *TI* 16 Se'71 7 : 1

Floods ravage Bihar; Halfhearted relief measures by govt. K. Gopalan *New Age* 19(33) 15 Ag'71 10

40 lakhs Bihar flood-hit facing starvation. *TI* 17 Ag'74
1 : 2-5+

450-metre rail track washed away on NER grand chord.
TI 9 Ag'71 1 : 4-5+

Ganga rises to record level : Battle on to save three Bihar
towns from flood ravages. *TI* 6 Ag'71 1 : 1-3+

Ghagra continues to rise above red mark. *TI* 12 Jl'75
1 : 7-8

Hundreds of villages inundated in Bihar. *TI* 22 Jl'71
7 : 1-2

Marooned villagers supplied with food by copters and army
boats. *TI* 11 Ag'71 3 : 3-4

Massive effort to repair breached NER track before
Dussehra. *TI* 11 Se'71 7 : 1-2

North Bihar flood situation critical. *TI* 30 Je'75 1 : 7-8

Parts of Monghyr and Chapra under water. *TI* 2 Ag'71
7 : 2-3

Patna town facing grave threat. *TI* 31 Jl'71 1 : 5-6+

Rivers on rampage again. *Commerce* 129(3301) 17 Ag'74
288-89

Threat again to Patna by Ganga floods. *TI* 20 Ag'71
7 : 4-5

38,850 sq. km in 12 Bihar Dists hit by floods. *TI* 24 Jl'71
7 : 6

2.5m. affected in 3 Bihar districts. *TI* 5 Se'75 1 : 7-8+

2,600 Bihar villages hit by floods. *TI* 12 Ag'75 1 : 1-2+

Worst-ever deluge in North Bihar. *TI* 9 Ag'75 1 : 1-3+

Wrong remedy; editorial. *TI* 14 Ag'75 4 : 1

   See also
Patna—Floods

FOLK art
  *Mithila ki samskrtik lokacitrakala. Lakshminath Jha.
  The author. (H). 1962, xxx, 179p. 28.5cm. Rs 33

  Sikki—Folk art of North-Bihar. D.S. Upadhyaya *Folklore*
  11(1) Ja'70 20-23

FOLK dancing
  Folk dances of Bihar. Hari Uppal *ill Wkly India* 89(11)
  17 Mr'68 22-25 ills

FOLK lore

*Bihar in folklore   study; an anthology with a general editorial from Sankar Sengupta. L.P. Vidyarathi and Ganesh Charley. Indian Pub. 1971, 312p. Rs 30

*Folk tales of Bihar. P.C. Roychaudhuri. Sahitya Akad. 1970, xxiv, 132p.   Rs 8

_____ : Bibliography

Addenda to a bibliography of folklore studies in Bihar. Gita Sengupta *Folklore* 11(12) De'70 452-71

A bibliography of folkloristic studies in Bihar : Books, articles, reports and monographs in English and Hindi. Harish Chandra Prasad *Folklore* 11(7) Jl'70   258-71; 11(9) Se'70 334-40; 11(10) Oc'71 369-83

FOLK songs

Around the koel and Kanhar, Pashupati Prasad Mahato *Folklore* 8(7) Jl'67 238-43

*Magahi samskar-git, Visvanathaprasad, *ed.* Bihar Rashtrabhasha Parishad. 1962, xxvi, 308p. ills map 24.5cm. Rs 6.50

Woodland verses. Subhendu Sekhar Bhattacharyya *Bull Cult Res Inst* 3(3-4) 1964 49-64

FOLK tales

*Bihar ki lok kathaem. Vatsa Sivmurtisimha. Atmaram. Pt. 2. 1961, vi, 52p. ills Rs 1.50

FOOD adulteration and inspection

Anti-adulteration scandal. *Link* 12(12) 2 Nv'69 17-18

FOOD supply

After Orissa, Bihar; editorial. *Eastern Econ* 47(20) 11 Nv'66 879-80

Bigger food crisis in offing in Bihar. K. Gopalan *New Age* 14(27) 3 Jl'66 6

Bihar govt. refuses to take strong steps. K. Gopalan *New Age* 12(26) 28 Je'64 11+

Bihar MLA's hunger-strike. K. Gopalan *New Age* 12(33) 16 Ag'64 10

Bihar's massive demonstration.   K. Gopalan   *New Age* 12(28) 12 Jl'64 10

CPI, SSP join hands for food struggle. K. Gopalan *New Age* 13(30) 25 Jl'65 5

Centre has failed Bihar. *New Age* 15(18) 30 Ap'67 3

Centre refuses to extend full help to Bihar. K. Gopalan *New Age* 15(20) 14 My'67 16

Deepening food crisis in Bihar. K. Gopalan *New Age* 21(20) 20 My'73 5

Embarrasment on food front. *Link* 8(10) 17 Oc'65 13-15

Famine conditions in villages. *Link* 7(48) 11 Jl'65 13-15

Famine under control; interview. Mahamaya Prasad Sinha *Yojana* 11(9) 14 My'67 2-4+

Food agitation continues in Bihar. K. Gopalan *New Age* 13(35) 29 Ag'65 4

Food campaign gains momentum in Bihar. K. Gopalan *New Age* 13(26) 27 Je'65 16

Food grains prices go up alarmingly. K. Gopalan *New Age* 13(21) 23 My'65 5

Food policy and its administration in Bihar. S.P. Sinha *Mainstream* 6(42) 15 Je'68 19-22

The foodgrains fiasco. A.K. Sen *Swarajya* 17(46) 12 My'73 19

Govt surrenders to food profiteers. K. Gopalan *New Age* 13(6) 7 Fe'65 8

Heated debate but no action. *Commerce* 115(2932) 22 Jl'67 180

Hoarders form the base for V.I.Ps. *Link* 7(22) 10 Ja'65 13

Hoarders' raj in Bihar : Curbs on stock holdings lifted, no price control. Indradeep Sinha *New Age* 13(30) 25 Jl'65 16

No rice in ration shops in Bihar : Procurement fiasco. Jitendra Singh *TI* 29 Ja'74 4 : 7-8

Opposition plans for mass agitation for food. K. Gopalan *New Age* 14(18) 1 My'66 7

People to begin dehoarding action. K. Gopalan *New Age* 13(31) 1 Ag'65 13

Prices shoot up in Bihar following centre's refusal to supply food. K. Gopalan *New Age* 15(30) 23 Jl'67 4

Serious danger of famine. *Link* 7(41) 23 My'65 19-21

A spectre is haunting Bihar. *econ and Political Wkly* 1(16) 3 De'66 655-66

Spectre of famine looms large over Bihar : K.B. Sahay in search of scapegoats to blame. K. Gopalan *New Age* 13(25) 20 Je'65 5+

FORESTS and forestry

*First working plan for the forests of Deoghar division in the district of Bhagalpur and Santhal Parganas, 1956-57 to 1965-66. Chief Conservator of Forests. xii, 103p.

*First working plan for the forests of Shahabad division, 1962-63 to 1971-72. Chief Conservator of Forests. 1963, 171p.

*First working plan for the Gaya forest division, Northern circle, Bihar, 1957-58 to 1966-67. Chief Conservator of Forests. xxii, 175p.

*First working plan for the Giridh Forest Division, Northern Circle, Bihar, 1957-58 to 1966-67. Chief Conservator of Forests. 1963, 290p.

*First working plan for the North Bihar Forest Division, Northern Circle, Bihar 1957-58 to 1966-67. Chief Conservator of Forests. x, 218p.

Forest conservation and lac in Bihar. S.P. Shahi *Foreign Trade of India* 13 My'64 48

Forests in Bihar. *Bihar Inform* 18(21) 16 De'70 7-8

*Fourth revised working plan for the reserved and protected forests of Saranda Division, Bihar, 1956-57 to 1975-76. Chief Conservator of Forests. 1962, vi, 259p.

Man and forest in Chotanagpur. Binay Kumar Rai *Vanyajati* 16(3) Jl'68 85-92

*Revised working plan for the reserved and protected forests of the Kolhan Division, Bihar, 1960-61 to 1975-76. Chief Conservator of Forests. 1963, xx, 167p.

*Revised working plan for the reserved forests of Koderma and Rajouli Ranges (Koderma and Gaya division), Bihar, 1959-60 to 1968-69. Chief Conservator of Forests. 1963, xvi, 70p.

*Revised working plan for the Santhal Pargana Division, 1955-56 to 1964-65. Chief Conservator of Forests, 1963, 178p.

*Revised working plan for the valley forests of Tribeni Block, Ganauli Range, Champaran Division, 1962-63 to 1971-72. Chief Conservator of Forests. 1963, iv, 35p.

The state's forest wealth. S.P. Shahi *ill Wkly India* 89(11) 17 Mr'68 45-46

*Working plan for the protected forests (vested under land reforms act, 1950) of Garhwar Division (Complete) and part of Palamau division for the period 1954-55 to 1963-64. Chief Conservator of Forests. 1962, xiv, 380p.

*Working plan for the protected forests (vested under land reforms act, 1950) of Gumla Division for the period, 1954-55 to 1965-66. Chief Conservator of Forests. 1961, xii, 194p.

*Working plan for the reserved and protected and private protected forests of Manbhum Divisions (as it existed prior to 1st Nov, 1956) now comprising Dhanbad Division of Bihar and Purulia Division of West Bengal, 1955-56 to 1964-65. 1962, x, 539p.

GANGULY, Bireshwar
Resource mobilisation in Bihar; 1951-73. *Commerce (Suppl)* 127(3263) 17 Nv'73   79-83   tabs   bibliogr

GARG, Kishore
Bihar movement is reaching out to uproot Indira's corruptocracy. *Organiser* 28(14) 16 Nv'74   3+

Jagjiwan poses increasing challenge to Indira. *Organiser* 28(1)   17 Ag'74   25+

GAUNTIA, R. and Sinha, V.N.P.
Trends in the urbanisation of the Chota Nagpur plateau. *Deccan Geographer* 7(2) Jl-De'69 117-28 tabs bibliogr

GAYA : History, Ancient
Members of medieval Brahmana family ruling in Gaya and their religious activities. Rama Chatterjee   *J Asiatic Soc (Bengal)* 7(1-2) 1965 7-11 bibliogr-ft-n

GHOSE, Basanta Chandra
The Neros and heroes of Bihar. *Janata* 29(10)   7 Ap'74 11-12

GHOSH, A.K.
For heavy industries, our own big machines. *Yojana* 8(21) 25 Oc'64   18-19

GHOSH, B.N.
The ways of acquiring mates in tribal Chotanagpur. *Folklore* 8(11)   Nv'67   403-10   bibliogr

GHOSH, Guru Charan
Middle phalangeal hair among certain groups of Bihar. *Man in India* 49(4) Oc-De'69 388-97 tabs bibliogr

GHOSH, Sankar
Jamshedpur's future : New climate of uncertainty. *TI* 9 Jl'70   6 : 3-5+

GHOSH, Somnath
Bihar movement—A democratic alternative in the making. *Janata* 29(22) 7 Jl'74   4

GIRI, V.V.

Handicrafts : A symbol of self reliance. *Bihar Inform* 16(21)   16 De'68   18-19

GOPALAN, K.

Anti-climax to toppling drama. *New Age* 15(39) 24 Se'67 4

Ayyangar forced to retire for not dismissing UF govt. *New Age* 15(50)   10 De'67   16+

Bigger food crisis in offing in Bihar.   *New Age*   14(27) 3 Jl'66   6

Bihar CPI conference.   *New Age*   12(50)   13 De'64   5   ills

Bihar CPI council reviews election results. *New Age* 17(14) 6 Ap'69   12+

Bihar : CPI holds its own fighting all alone. *New Age* 19(12)   21 Mr'71   7

Bihar CPI joins ministry to thwart Congress come-back. *New Age*   16(19)   12 My'68   16

Bihar : CPI plans mass campaign.   *New Age*   19(17) 25 Ap'71   7

Bihar CPI vote goes up by 60 per cent.   *New Age*   17(8) 23 Fe'69   4

Bihar : CPI warns against. Congress-R machinations. *New Age*   19(29)   18 Jl'71   16

Bihar : CPM aligns with Syndicate-Jana Sangh.   *New Age* 20(9)   27 Fe'72   8

Bihar Congress backs out from commitments. *New Age* 19(7)   14 Fe'71   8-9

Bihar Congress bid to reduce elections to farce.   *New Age* 15(7)   12 Fe'67   6

Bihar Congress coalition evokes all round contempt.   *New Age*   17(11)   16 Mr'69   7

Bihar Congress hatching plot against U.F. govt.   *New Age* 15(16)   16 Ap'67   3+

Bihar Congress plans to form post-election coalition. *New Age* 17(2)   12 Ja'69   7

Bihar : Congress resorts to pressure tactics.   *New Age*   19(6) 7 Fe'71   7

Bihar conspirators in desperate mood.   *New Age*   16(4) 28 Ja'68   11

Bihar efforts to forge left united front.   *New Age*   16(38) 22 Se'68   7

Bihar govt. refuses to take strong steps. *New Age* 12(26) 28 Je'64 11+

Bihar government takes some progressive steps : But land-lord pressure continues. *New Age* 20(27) 2 Jl'72 13

Bihar Governor outlines Front's programme, policies. *New Age* 15(13) 26 Mr'67 6 ill

Bihar : Initial steps for left unity. *New Age* 16(30) 28 Jl'68 5

Bihar Khet Mazdoor Sabha plans agitation. *New Age* 13(24) 13 Je'65 6

Bihar : Kulak lobby in action. *New Age* 20(20) 14 My'72 16

Bihar MLA's hunger-strike. *New Age* 12(33) 16 Ag'64 10

Bihar miners gain assurance on bonus. *New Age* 13(15) 11 Ap'65 6

Bihar miners serve bonus strike notice. *New Age* 14(13) 27 Mr'66 6

Bihar ministry collapse inevitable. *New Age* 16(9) 3 Mr'68 9

Bihar's massive demonstration. *New Age* 12(28) 12 Jl'64 10

Bihar NGO leader victimised, ban on processions imposed. *New Age* 13(12) 21 Mr'65 9

Bihar NGO strike is withdrawn. *New Age* 16(31) 4 Ag'68 7

Bihar NGO struggle enters new stage. *New Age* 13(10) 7 Mr'65 9

Bihar ordinance ready to limit property holdings. *New Age* 19(32) 8 Ag'71 3

Bihar prepares for party Congress. *New Age* 16(3) 21 Ja'68 5+

Bihar : Reaction fails to forge united front. *New Age* 20(8) 20 Fe'72 11

Bihar SSP men fight like kilkenny cats. *New Age* 19(5) 31 Ja'71 5

Bihar teachers win demands. *New Age* 19(20) 16 My'71 7

Bihar UF alerts people about Bengal-model coup. *New Age* 15(50) 10 De'67 4

Bihar UF govt. to protect tenants. *New Age* 15(42) 15 Oc'67 7

Bihar UF ministry falls victim to conspiracy. *New Age* 16(5) 4 Fe'68   4+

Bihar uncertainty persists.   *New Age* 18(50)   13 De'70   7

Bihar universities face crisis—Staff on strike. *New Age* 17(7) 27 Ap'69   4

Bihar : Unjustified claims of CP(M).   *New Age*   14(52) 25 De'66   8-9

Bills to lower ceilings and limit urban property.   *New Age* 19(27)   4 Jl'71   3

Bureaucrats plot sabotage of Aiyar commission work. *New Age* 16(37)   15 Se'68   4

CPI welcomes midterm election in Bihar.   *New Age*   20(1) 2 Ja'72   11

CPI, SSP join hands for food struggle.   *New Age*   13(30) 25 Jl'65   5

CPI's big growth in strength and influence in Bihar.   *New Age* 16(44)   3 Nv'68   4

Centre refuses to extend full help to Bihar. *New Age* 15(20) 14 My'67   16

Centre's antipathy forced Bihar to declare famine. *New Age* 15(18)   30 Ap'67   11

Congress dissidents still at toppling game. *New Age* 18(47) 22 Nv'70   6

Congress plots for central intervention in Bihar.   *New Age* 15(25)   18 Je'67   16+

Congressmen quarrel while Bihar starves. *New Age* 14(48) 27 Nv'66   7

Deepening food crisis in Bihar. *New Age* 21(20) 20 My'73 5

Exodus from Bihar Congress camp.   *New Age*   15(3) 15 Ja'67   16

Explosive situation in adivasi areas of Bihar.   *New Age* 16(25)   23 Je'68   8-9

Famine grips Bihar.   *New Age*   14(45)   6 Nv'66   4

Feud in Bihar Congress over spoils of power.   *New Age* 17(17)   27 Ap'69   7+

Floods ravage Bihar—Halfhearted relief measures by govt. *New Age* 19(33)   15 Ag'71   10

Food agitation continues in Bihar.   *New Age*   13(35) 29 Ag'64   4

Food campaign gains momentum in Bihar. *New Age* 13(26) 27 Je'65   16

Food grains prices go up alarmingly. *New Age*   13(21) 23 My'65   5

Food riots, starvation deaths in Bihar : Government remains passive and complacent. *New Age* 13(28) 11 Jl'65 1+

Govt surrenders to food profiteers. *New Age* 13(6) 7 Fe'65 8

Index fraud in Bihar exposed : AITUC demands tripartite investigation committee. *New Age* 13(10) 7 Mr'65 5

Masses act against price rise. *New Age* 14(15) 10 Ap'66 7

New pay scale fail to meet NGO's demand. *New Age* 13(27) 4 Jl'65   6

No confidence against Pande Ministry. *New Age* 21(23) 10 Je'73   16

Not only repression, more taxes in Bihar. *New Age* 13(43) 24 Oc'65   10

Officials hamper Bihar government's massive famine relief operation. *New Age* 15(22) 28 My'67 8-9

Operation role—Back succeeds in Bihar. *New Age* 16(12) Mr'68   2

Opposition plans for mass agitation for food. *New Age* 14(18) 1 Mr'66 7

Party firmly united in Bihar : Assessment of district conference. *New Age* 12(48) 1 Nv'64 20

People to begin dehoarding action. *New Age* 13(31) 1 Ag'65   13

People's victory in Bihar—Congress plot smashed. *New Age* 15(32) 6 Ag'67 16

Prices shoot up in Bihar following centre's refusal to supply food. *New Age* 15(30) 23 Jl'67 4

Quit or face no-confidence : Rebel's ultimatum to Bihar Congress bosses. *New Age* 15(29) 16 Jl'67 12

Reactionary SVD raj in Bihar tumbles. *New Age* 19(23) 6 Je'71   16

Rs 5.5 crores new taxes in Bihar : Mass protest before Assembly on March 1 planned. *New Age* 14(8) 20 Fe'66 6

Sahay insists using DIR against opposition parties. *New Age* 14(14) 3 Ap'66 5

Sahay Ministry indicted : Debate on no-confidence motion. *New Age* 12(34) 23 Ag'64 2

Sahay's authoritarian regime must end. *New Age* 15(4) 22 Ja'67 2

Spectre of famine looms large over Bihar : K.B. Sahay in search of scapegoats to blame. *New Age* 13(25) 20 Je'65 5+

Swatantra entry upsets Congress power balance. *New Age* 12(39) 27 Se'64 7

Tata zamindari goes : New bill passed in Bihar Assembly. *New Age* 20(26) 25 Je'72 7

Tata zamindari to go. *New Age* 15(34) 20 Ag'67 4

Violence—Main plank of reaction in Bihar. *New Age* 19(11) 14 Mr'71 3

Wind in Bihar favours left democratic forces. *New Age* 19(9) 28 Fe'71 10

GORAY, N.G.

Bihar and the democratic machinery. *Janata* 29(31) 15 Se'74 8-10

Movement of the masses. *Janata* 29(41) 17 Nv-24 Nv'74 9-12

GOVERNMENT advertising

Ethics of government advertizing; editorial. *Thought* 26(16) 27 Ap'74 5-6

GOVERNORS

A Governor takes leave. *Commerce* 115(2952) 9 De'67 1369-70

Governors and Deputy-Governors of Bihar in the eighteenth century. K.K. Datta *Bengal Past & Present* 81(1) Ja-Je'62 32-36 ft-n

GOVINDRAO, Despande

Jayaprakash Narayan on Bihar—A citizen action pamphlet. 1970, 38p. Rs 2 Review *Commerce* 129(3298) 27 Jl'74 179

GRAIN

Growth of food grain production in Bihar. S.A. Khan *Indian J agric Econ* 24(2) Ap-Je'69 94-99 tabs ft-n

A study of trends and variations in the prices of foodgrains in Bihar with special reference to prices of cereals between 1956 and 1968. Surendra Prasad Sinha and Benoy Nath Varma *Indian J agric Econ* 26(4) Oc-De'71 446-47

GRANTS-in-aid

Finance Commission and grants-in-aid : The case of Bihar. R.K. Sinha *Commerce* 127(3263) 17 Nv'73 67-69

GULATI, Hans Raj

The challenge of Bihar. *Janata* 29(35) 13 Oc'74 8-9

Trade unions must join the struggle. *Janata* 29(39) 10 Nv'74 5

GUPTA, D.D.

Hazaribagh : "Land of a thousand gardens." *Bihar Inform* 18(4) 1 Mr'70 21-22

GUPTA, Devidas

The satyagraha in Champaran. *Bihar Inform* 18(14) 15 Ag'70 45-47

GUPTA, Dipankar

Poll prospects Chotanagpur : New equations in changed situation. *Mainstream* 9(23) 6 Fe'71 12-13+

GUPTA, P.L.

Ancient handicrafts. *Marg* 20(1) De'66 13-15

GUPTA, Ranjit

The Musahri project. *Voluntary Action* 14(4-5) Jl-Oc'72 3-19 tabs

Rural-urban industries project. *Voluntary Action* 15(4-5) Jl-Oc'73 17-32

GUPTA, Satya Prakash

Adibasi 'Handia' beverage. *Adibasi* 12(1-4) Ap'70-Ja'71 123-26 bibliogr

HAIR

Middle phalangeal hair among certain groups of Bihar. Guru Charan Ghosh *Man in India* 49(4) Oc-De'69 388-97 tabs bibliogr

HALDAR, Asesh Kumar

Kharia birth statistics of Nawatoli. *Vanyajati* 19(2-3) Ap-Jl'71 tabs bibliogr

HANDICRAFTS

Ancient handicrafts. P.L. Gupta *Marg* 20(1) De'66 13-15

Art and crafts. U. Maharathi *ill Wkly India* 89(12) 24 Mr'68 40-41

Handicrafts : A symbol of self-reliance. V.V. Giri *Bihar Inform* 16(21) 16 De'68 18-19

HANDLOOM industry and trade

Handloom industry of Manpur (Gaya) : A survey. N.C. Agrawal *Indian J Commerce* 23(3) Se'70 87-95

Problems of handloom industry. *Link* 7(23) 17 Ja'65 26

HARBHAJAN SINGH, S.

Bihar—Setting a pattern for agitation. *Janata* 29(31) 15 Se'74 4-5

HARI PRAKASH

  See Desai, D.K. jt. auth.

HARIHAR SINGH

Harihar mirrors Congress rot. Pauly V. Parakal *New Age* 17(9) 2 Mr'69 2

HAZARIBAGH

Hazaribagh : "Land of a thousand gardens." D.D. Gupta *Bihar Inform* 18(4) 1 Mr'70 21-22

HEAVY Engineering Corporation, Ranchi

Assessing the prospects for Heavy Engineering Corporation. K.S. Ramachandran *Capital* 162(4043) 2 Ja'69 19-20

Big wage hike for technical staff. *Indian Worker* 18(11) 15 De'69 8-9

Enquiry report disclosures. *Capital* 153(3831) 8 Oc'64 562-63

Failure of management in Ranchi. *Eastern Econ* 43(22) 27 Nv'64 1025

For heavy industries, our own big machines. A.K. Ghosh *Yojana* 8(21) 25 Oc'64 18-19

HEC : A sorry tale; editorial. *Eastern Econ* 58(20) 19 My'72 964

HEC makes progress despite delayed delivery schedules. K.D. Malaviya *Capital* 162(4046) 23 Ja'69 143-45

HEC marches ahead. C. Chalapati Rao *Bihar Inform* 17(15) 1 Se'69 18+; *Indian Fin* 84(7) 16 Ag'69 192

HEC of Ranchi. *Yojana* 7(24) 8 De'63 3-5

HEC on the mat. *econ Wkly* 16(15) 11 Ap'64 671-72

HEC record in 1967-68. *Indian Fin* 84(7) 16 Ag'69 210

HEC to yield revenue in four years. *TI* 10 Ja'69 11 : 4-5

HEC's role in setting up the Bokaro Steel Plant. C. Chalapati Rao *Capital (Suppl)* 163(4070) 10 Jl'69 87-88

Heavy Engineering Corporation : Estimates Committee report highly critical. *Commerce* 108(2765) 18 Ap'64 654-55

Heavy Engineering Corporation in a mess. Subhash J. Rele *Swarajya* 17(5) 29 Jl'72 9-10

Heavy Engineering Corporation Limited. *econ Stud* 10(2) Ag'69 163-64

Heavy Engineering Corporation, Ranchi. *Indian Architect* 6(7) Jl'64 15-18 ills

Philosophy out of fire. *econ Wkly* 16(41) 10 Oc'64 1632-33

Ranchi HEC fire was result of sabotage. *New Age* 12(41) 11 Oc'64 2

Sabotage in Ranchi? *Organiser* 17(27) 10 Fe'64 1-2

600 engineers of HEC, Ranchi want to resign and leave the country. *Organiser* 22(41) 24 My'69 4+

Thinking big and looking forward. *Yojana* 7(24) 8 De'63 6

Third mystery fire in Ranchi. *Organiser* 18(6) 21 Se'64 1-2

HIGH Court : Decisions

Constitution of India, articles 7 and 5—Migration and domicile minor can migrate independently—Article 7 over-rides article 5. K.R.N. Nambiar *Indian J int Law* 7(4) Oc'67 553-56

Labour decision and settlement : Decision—The decision of the High Court of Patna in the dispute between the management of Toposi Colliery and their workmen and others *Indian Lab J* 8(5) My'67 441-43

Labour decision and settlement : Decision—The decision of the High Court of Judicature at Patna in the dispute between Tata Iron and Steel Company Ltd. and Hirangi and others *Indian Lab J* 8(10) Oc'67 819-20

Labour decision and settlement : Decision—The decision of the High Court of Judicature at Patna in the disputes between Tata Iron and Steel Company Ltd. and workmen of Tata Iron and Steel Company Ltd. (in relation to Bhelatand Sijua Collieries). *Indian Lab J* 8(6) Je'67 523-24

HISTORICAL geography

Historical geography of Bihar on the eve of the early Turkish invasions. Hasan Nishat Ansari *J Bihar Res Soc* 49 Ja-De'68 253-60

HISTORY

Beginnings of modern education in Mithila. Jatashankar Jha. K.P. Jayaswal Res Inst. 1972, 256p. Rs 18 Review *J Indian Hist* 52(2-3) Ag-De'74 498-500

Historical-cultural heritage. J.C. Mathur *Marg* 20(1) De'66 4-12 ills

*History of Bihar. Radhakrsna Caudhuri. Madhipura. Shanti Devi. 1958, x, 421. pls bibliogr 22cm. Rs 12.50

The Lichchavis (of Vaisdi). Hit Narayan Jha. Chowkhamba Sk. 1970, ixvi, 248p. Rs 25 Review *J Bihar Res Soc* 58(1-4) Ja-De'72 321-22

    See also

Indigo workers—History

Patna—History

HISTORY, Ancient

The Mandar hill : A general survey. Adhay Kant Choudhary *J Bihar Res Soc* 50(1-4) Ja-De'64 32-42 bibliogr

A note on the topography of ancient Rajariha. Madan Mohan Singh *J Bihar Res Soc* 50(1-4) Ja-De'64 23-26 bibliogr-ft-n

Rice and fall of the Vrijjian Republic. R. Balchand *Bihar Inform* 18(2) 26 Ja'70 4-8

    See also

Antiquities

Gaya—History, Ancient

Inscriptions

HISTORY, Medieval

Bihar affairs in 1756-58. K.K. Datta *J Indian Hist* 40(3) De'62 781-801 bibliogr

History of Bihar (1740-1772). Govind Misra. Munshiram. 187p. Rs 22 Review *TI* 1 Ag'71 10 : 5-6

The Khandavalas of Mithila. Radhakrishna Chaudhary *J Bihar Res Soc (Sec II)* 48 Ja-De'62 41-63

Mithila and Nepal. Luciano Petech *J Bihar Res Soc (Sec III)* 48 Ja-De'62 13-18 bibliogr

The Nagbansis and the Choros. B. Virottam. Munshiram. 1972, 224p. Rs 29 Review *Indian Arch* 22(1-2) Ja-De'73 117-18

Sanskrit learning in Mithila under the Khandavala dynasty.
Upendra Thakur *J Bihar Res Soc (Sec III)* 48 Ja-De'62
90-104

Socio-economic life in Mithila under the Khandavalas.
Upendra Thakur *J Bihar Res Soc (Sec III)* 48 Ja-De'62
64-89 ft-n

Tirhut (North Bihar) and Bihar (South Bihar) under
Muhammad Tughluq : A.D. 1325-1351. Hasan Nishat
Ansari *J Bihar Res Soc* 50(1-4) Ja-De'64 59-72 bibliogr

A view of the provincial administration of Bihar under
Farrukhsiyar, 1712-19. Qeyamuddin Ahmad *J Bihar Res
Soc* 50(1-4) Ja-De'64 114-24

HISTORY, Modern

*The administration of justice under the East-India Com-
pany in Bengal, Bihar and Orissa. Atulcandra Patra. Asia.
1962, viii, 233p. 21.5cm. Rs 10

The creation of Santhal Parganas. P.C Roy Chaudhry
Bengal Past & Present 81(1) Ja-Je'62 50 56

Governors and Deputy-Governors of Bihar in the eighteenth
century. K.K. Datta *Bengal Past & Present* 81(1) Ja-Je'62
32-36 ft-n

Militant nationalism in Bihar (1900-1920). Nagendra
Mohan Prasad Srivastava *Mainstream* 10(48) 29 Jl'72
35-39 bibliogr

Raja Arjun Singh of Porahat. Pratap Narayan Jha *J
Historical Res* 15(2) 26 Ja'73 92-100 bibliogr-ft-n

The role of Mahatma Gandhi in the creation of renascent
Bihar. *J Indian Hist* 47(3) De'69 457-70 bibliogr-ft-n

The struggle for freedom. Sachchidananda *ill Wkly India*
89(11) 17 Mr'68 15-17 ills

    See also

Birsa

HOUSING

Housing scandal. *Link* 12(2) 24 Ag'69 19-20

Large scale housing through revolving fund. *Bihar Inform*
18(11) 16 Je'70 9-11

Number of houses in Bihar go up by 21 percent. *TI*
22 Ap'70 5 : 4

HOUSING, Cooperative

In Bihar, co-op. housing on the move. *Janata (Independence
Day Number)* 30(25) 1975 18

HYGIENE, Rural

A health survey of kamrr village, Ranchi. L.P. Vidyarthi and P. Dash Sharma *J soc Res* 16(1) Mr'73 82-86 tabs appdx

ILLITERACY

Literacy in Singhbhum, Bihar. Maya Banerjee *Geographical Rev India* 37(2) Je'75 151-57 tabs bibliogr

INDIAN National Congress : Bihar unit

Battle of Sadaqat Ashram. *Link* 12(14) 16 Nv'69 17

Bihar : Amity in the offing ? *Link* 4(41) 20 My'62 19-20

Bihar C.M. directed to exclude Ramgarh from cabinet. *TI* 14 Mr'69 1 : 1-5

Bihar Congress coalition evokes all round contempt. K. Gopalan *New Age* 17(11) 16 Mr'69 7

Bihar's new Chief. *Link* 5(4) 2 Se'62 13

Congressmen quarrel while Bihar starves. K. Gopalan *New Age* 14(48) 27 Nv'66 7

Exodus from Bihar Congress camp. K. Gopalan *New Age* 15(3) 15 Ja'67 16

Feud in Bihar Congress over spoils of power. K. Gopalan *New Age* 17(17) 27 Ap'69 7+

High Command for replacement of Bihar Assembly party leader. *TI* 6 Jl'69 9 : 4-5

High Command's concern at Bihar leader's role. *TI* 5 Fe'69 4 : 3-4

Indiscipline in Bihar. *Link* 5(43) 2 Jl'63 15

New grouping in Bihar. *Link* 6(37) 26 Ap'64 13

M.P. Sinha blames High Command for reverses in Bihar. *TI* 13 Mr'69 5 : 4-5

Top leaders boycott PCC executive. *TI* 9 Mr'69 1 : 8

INDIAN National Congress (New) : Bihar unit

Bihar Cong-N leader election on March 29. *TI* 27 Mr'71 9 : 3-4

Bihar Congress Party in disarray. *TI* 16 Oc'74 1 : 2-5+

Bihar : Politics of spoils. *Link* 16(18) 9 De'73 20-21

Bogus members pack Bihar Cong-1. *Organiser* 26(14) 11 Nv'72 7

Congress in coma. *Link* 12(48) 28 Je'70 15-16

Crisis deepens in Bihar Congress. *TI* 6 My'73 5 : 2-3

Fissures reappear in Bihar Congress. *TI* 25 My'73 7 : 1-2

List of Congress candidates for Bihar Assembly poll. *TI*
7 Fe'72 4 : 1-3

Many lessons for the Bihar Congress. *Link* 15(40)
13 My'73 17-18

Mess in Bihar. *Link* 16(38) 28 Ap'74 15

Mishra for review of Congress-CPI relations in Bihar. *TI*
21 Ap'73 1 : 7-8+

New look adhoc Congress body for Bihar. *TI* 27 Se'71
1 : 2-5+

Paswan's colleagues in former Cabinet get Congress ticket.
TI 7 Fe'72 1 : 7-8+

INDIAN National Congress (Organisation) : Bihar unit
Bosses at bay. *Link* 12(15) 23 Nv'69 17-19

Desperate moves. *Link* 12(9) 12 Oc'69 15-16

Looking for lead from Lucknow. *Commerce* 119(3056)
29 Nv'69 1050

Pro-PM chief of Bihar PCC replaced. *TI* 20 Nv'69
1 : 5-6+

Rival Congress groups meet at Patna this month. *TI*
7 Nv'69 9 : 1-2

Syndicate group bid foiled in Bihar. *TI* 9 Nv'69 6 : 5

Tripathi and A.P. Sharma among 14 'removed'. *TI*
1 De'69 1 : 1+

INDIAN National Trade Union Congress : Bihar unit
Engineering wage board report : Early govt. decision
demanded. *Indian Worker* 17(25) 24 Mr'69 1+

INDIGO workers : History
The satyagraha in Champaran. Devidas Gupta *Bihar
Inform* 18(14) 15 Ag'70 45-47

The stain of Indigo and birth of satyagraha in India. Razi
Ahmad *Bihar Inform* 18(14) 15 Ag'70 24-28

INDRA KUMAR
Banking by State Government. *Mankind* 13(1) Ja-Fe'69
31-32

INDUSTRIAL relations
Code of discipline and industrial peace in Bihar. Daroga
Prasad Roy *Indian Lab J* 4(3) Mr'63 237-39

Security guards, police attack Bhilai workers. Satish Loomba *New Age* 15(28) 9 Jl'67 6

Settlement in Bihar mines. *New Age* 15(28) 9 Jl'67 6

INDUSTRIES

Accelerating industrial growth. *Commerce* 125(3216) 23 De'72 1526

Bihar's state income and industrialization. Subhash Chandra Sarkar *mod Rev* 127(3) Se'70 179-84 tabs bibliogr-ft-n

Bihar's 'war on administrative delays.' *Commerce* 125(3197) 12 Ag'72 389-91

FICCI chief for single agency for approving new industrial units. *TI* 5 Fe'72 2 : 5-6

The impact of industrialisation in lower Ghaghara Gandak Doab. Rama Shanker Lal *Deccan Geographer* 12(2) Jl-De'74 117-26 map

Industrial awakening in Bihar. K. Sundararaman *Eastern Econ* 40(22) 7 Je'63 1313-14

Industrial development. K. Suresh Singh *Commerce (Suppl)* 117(3263) 17 Nv'73 41-44

Industrial profile of states-3—Bihar : Politics hinders development. Subhash Chandra Sarkar *Commerce (Annual Number)* 117(3009) 1968 240-45 tab

*Industrial programmes for fourth plan; Bihar. NCAER. 1967, x, 205p. Rs 20

Industrialisation of Bihar. Kedar Pandey *Bihar Inform* 18(10) 1 Je'70 1-2

Manufacturing regions of North-Bihar. Bishweshwar Mandal *nat Geographical J India* 17(1) Mr'71 51-62 bibliogr-ft-n

Opportunities for industrial growth. A.F. Couto *Commerce (Suppl)* 127(3263) 17 Nv'73 31-39

Opportunities of development. R.T. Sinha *Link* 7(23) 17 Ja'65 23-24

The pattern of industry. G.P. Sinha *ill Wkly India* 89(12) 24 Mr'68 14-15

Processing industries and their role in a rural economy; a case study. Surendra Prasad Sinha *AICC econ Rev* 18(23) 15 Je'67 23-25+ tabs

Push to big industries in Bihar. *Eastern Econ* 40(7) 22 Fe'63 326

Rural electrification and industrial development of North Bihar. Raj Kishore Sinha *Bihar Inform* 18(12) 1 Je'70 8+

Rural-urban industries project. Ranjit Gupta *Voluntary Action* 15(4-5) Jl-Oc'73 17-32 tabs appdx

Some growth points for the development of chemical and allied industries in Bihar. S.M. Prasad *Bihar Inform* 18(2) 26 Ja'70 31-32

Strategy of industrial growth. Chandra Shekhar Singh *Commerce (Suppl)* 127(3263) 17 Nv'73 7-11

Unfruitful deliberations. *Commerce* 115(2947) 4 Nv'67 1066-67

    See also

Cottage industries

Cotton powerloom industry and trade

Fertilizer industry and trade

Handloom industry and trade

Khadi industry and trade

Pharmaceutical industry and trade

Rural industries

Seed industry and trade

Silk manufacture and trade

Small-scale industries

Sugar industry and trade

_____ : Finance

Institutional financing of industrial development in Bihar. C.D. Singh and M.L. Sharma *Southern Econ* 13(15) 1 De'74 11-13 tabs

_____ : History

    See also

Opium industry and trade : History

_____ : Statistics

Industrial structure of Bihar : 1969. *Commerce (Suppl)* 127(3263) 17 Nv'73 89

INDUSTRY and state

Bihar Chief Minister's industry plan favours private sector. *New Age* 20(39) 24 Se'72 1+

Industrial policy for fifth plan. S.P. Thakur *Commerce (Suppl)* 127(3263) 17 Nv'73 77-78

Industrialisation in Bihar : Incentives and prospects. R.L. Bishnoi *Bihar Inform* 18(2) 26 Ja'70 19-21

K.B.'s problems. *Link* 6(14) 17 Nv'63 23-24

INLAND water transportation

Scope for developing water transport services in Bihar. *Capital* 167(4189) 18 Nv'71 935-36

INSCRIPTIONS

Bihar stone pillar inscriptions—A revised study. I. Karthikeya Sarma *J orient Inst* 17(3) Mr'68 267-74 bibliogr

*Select inscriptions of Bihar. Radhakrsna Caudhari. Shanta Devi. 1958, 54, 138p. 18cm. Rs 10.50

So-Called Bihar stone pillar inscription of Shandagupta. S.V. Sohani *J Bihar Res Soc* 49 Ja-De'63 170-77 bibliogr-ft-n

Some observations on the Bihar stone pillar inscription. Jagannath Agarwal *J orient Inst* 20(1) Se'70 44-47 bibliogr-ft-n

INTELLECTUAL life

Some forgotton literatures of Mithila. Trilokanatha Jha *J Bihar Res Soc (Soc III)* 48 Ja-De'62 54-60 ft-n

IRRIGATION

Bihar : Big projects, big problems. *Yojana* 12(13) 7 Jl'68 39-42 ills

Evaluation of irrigation schemes in Palamau district (Bihar) : A case study. M.L. Singh and P.K. Prasad *Indian J agric Econ* 28(4) Oc-De'73 235-36

Irrigation in Bihar. Narsingh Baitha *Bihar Inform* 18(11) 16 Je'70 3-4

Problems of irrigation. *Bihar Inform* 18(19) 16 Nv'70 4-7

Riots over water feared in Shahabad district. *TI* 10 Ap'70 11 : 3

Vaishali blazes a trail again. B.P. Chaturvedi *Bihar Inform* 18(21) 16 De'70 1+

IYER GOPAL, K.

See Sachchidananda jt. auth.

JAIN, Girilal

Strangulation of Bihar : Need for a rescue operation. *TI* 10 Jl'74 4 : 3-5

JAIN, H.M.

Implications of Mandal drama. *Mainstream* 6(26) 24 Fe'68 13-14

JAIN, P.K. and Sharma, B.B.L.

A micro study of motivators in Bihar vasectomy camps. *Voluntary Action* 16(6) Nv-De'74 13-14

JAIN, Yaspal, *ed.*

*Pataliputra. Sasta Sahitya Mandal. 1959, 30p. 18cm. Re 0.37

JAISWAL, N.K.

See Ambastha, C.K. jt. auth.; Jha, P.P. jt. auth.

_____ and Ambastha, C.K.

Caste and occupational preference in East Bihar villages. *Indian J soc Wk* 31(2) Jl'70 191-95 tabs

_____ and Chouhan, K.N.K.

People's perception of village panchayat under panchayati raj. *quart J Local Self-Government Inst* 41(3) Ja-Mr'71 267-73

_____ and others

Agricultural extension programme : How rural leaders and followers look at it. *quart J Local Self-Government Inst* 42(1) Jl-Se'71 63-72 tabs

_____ and Vyas, U.K.

Impact of Kosi embankment : A study of two villages in North Bihar. *econ and Political Wkly* 4(47) 22 Nv'69 1821-22 tabs

JAMSHEDPUR

Physical basis of the city of Jamshedpur—An urban study. Ashok Kumar Dutt *Deccan Geographer* 3(1) Ja'65 1-10 bibliogr

_____ : Social conditions

Modernisation and social structure : Family, caste and class in Jamshedpur. Michael M. Ames *econ and Political Wkly* 4(28-30) Jl'69 1217-24 tab

*Report on socio-economic survey of Jamshedpur city. Univ of Patna (Dept. of Applied Economics and Commerce). 1959. Rs 10

JANA Sangh : Bihar unit

Bihar BJS defence conference : A huge success. *Organiser* 19(20) 2 Ja'66 11

25 of 34 Bihar MLAs boycotted PSP's historic session. *Organiser* 17(44) 1 Je'64 16

JANAK SINGH

Bihar's abysmal poverty : Millions in bondage. *TI* 23 Se'74 4 : 7-8

JAYAPRAKASH NARAYAN

Face to face. *Khadi Gramodyog* 17(3) De'70 201-08; *Voluntary Action* 8(1-2) Ja-Ap'71 3-11

The problem of self-renewal in Bihar. *Commerce (Suppl)* 127(3263) 17 Nv'73 3-5

Under the pretext of fighting Naxalite-Open collusion between administration and landlords. *Janata* 30(17) 1 Je'75 2+

Why students should sacrifice one year of studies. *Organiser* 27(50) 27 Jl'74 8-9

JHA, Bhogendra

Bihar peasants fight back govt. onslaughts. *New Age* 12(4) 26 Ja'64 16

JHA, Binodananda

The adivasi problem in Bihar. *Link (Annual Number)* 5(1) 15 Ag'62 39

JHA, Chetakar

Election panorama in Bihar. *Political Sci Rev* 6(3-4)-7(1-2) Jl-Se'67-Ap-Je'68 139-51 tabs

——— and Jha, Shree Nagesh

Some aspects of Bihar politics. *India quart* 20(3) Jl-Se'64 312-29 tabs bibliogr-ft-n

JHA, D.

Structure, employment and earnings of agricultural labour in Champaran district in Bihar. *Indian J agric Econ* 25(3) Jl-Se'70 64-65

——— and Salunke, S.D.

Land tenure system and capital formation in agriculture; summary. *Indian J agric Econ* 24(4) Oc-De'69 130-31

JHA, D.N.

Bihar's fifth plan : An appraisal. *Southern Econ* 13(4) 15 Je'74 19-21

Planning and agricultural development. S. Chand. 1974, 232p. Rs 30 Review
Indian J industr Relations 10(4) Ap'75 615-17

JHA, Dayanatha

Acreage response of sugarcane in factory areas of North Bihar. *Indian J agric Econ* 25(1) Ja-Mr'70 79-91 tabs bibliogr-ft-n

_____ and Maji, C.C.

Cobweb phenomenon and fluctuations in sugarcane acreage in North Bihar. *Indian J agric Econ* 26(4) Oc-De'71 415-21 fig

JHA, Divakar

*Bihar finances (1912-13 to 1960-61). Granthamala karyalaya. 1963, x, 393p. tabs bibliogr 22cm. Rs 15

Economics of crop pattern of irrigated farms in North Bihar. *Indian J agric Econ* 18(1) Ja-Mr'63 168-69 tabs

JHA, Hit Narayan

The Lichchacis (of Vaisdi). Chowkhamba Sk. 1970, ixvi, 248p. Rs 25 Review
J Bihar Res Soc 58(1-4) Ja-De'72 321-22

JHA, J C.

History of land revenue of Chota-Nagpur in the first half of the 19th century. *J Bihar Res Soc* 50(1-4) Ja-De'64 105-13

See also Sarkar, J.N. jt. auth.

JHA, Jagdish Narayan

See Sarkar, Jagdish Narayan. jt. auth.

JHA, Jatashankar

Baginnings of modern education in Mithila. K.P. Jayaswal Res Inst. 1972, 256p. Rs 18 Review
J Indian Hist 52(2-3) Ag-De'74 498-500

Early printing presses and newspapers in Bihar. *J Bihar Res Soc* 50(1-4) Ja-De'64 98-104

JHA, Jivanath

*Janakapur paricaya. Darbhanga press co., ii, 34p. ills 21.5cm. Rs 1.25

JHA, Lakshminath

*Mithila ki samskrtik lokacitrakala. The author. 1962, xxx, 179p. col. pls 28.5cm. Rs 33

JHA, M.N.

See Sinha, S.P. jt. auth.

JHA, Modnath

See Sinha, Surendra Prasad. jt. auth.

JHA, Nagesh

Bye-election in a Bihar Assembly Constituency : Study in voting behaviour. *econ and Political Wkly* 1(10) 22 Oc'66 417-20 tabs

Caste in Bihar politics. *econ and Political Wkly* 5(7) 14 Fe'70 341-44 tabs

JHA, P.P. and Jaiswal, N.K.

Social distance between scheduled castes and upper castes in East Bihar villages. *Bihar Inform* 17(21) 16 De'69 4-6

JHA, Pratap Narayan

Raja Arjun Singh of Porahat. *J Historical Res* 15(2) 26 Ja'73 92-100 bibliogr-ft-n

JHA, Prem Shankar

Far too many controls : Formidable bias against investment. *TI* 29 Ag'74 4 : 3-5

JHA, S.K.

Bihar scene-the politics of suspended animation. *J soc Stud State Govts* 2(3) Jl-Se'69 171-73

JHA, Satish Chandra

Levels of living in rural household. *Indian J agric Econ* 18(1) Ja-Mr'63 311-16

JHA, Shashishekhar

Political elite in Bihar. Vora. 1972, 332p. Rs 25 Review *Commerce* 125(3212) 25 Nv'72 1347; *Eastern Econ* 59(9) 1 Se'72 508; *Indian and Foreign Rev* 10(14) 1 My'73 20-21

Tribal leadership in Bihar. *econ and Political Wkly* 3(15) 13 Ap'68 603-08

JHA, Shree Nagesh

See Jha, Chetakar. jt. auth.

JHA, Trilokanatha

Some forgotton literatures of Mithila. *J Bihar Res Soc (Soc III)* 48 Ja-De'62 54-60 ft-n

JHARKAND Party

Jharkand is alive. *Link* 8(18) 12 De'65 14

JITENDRA SINGH

Bihar coalition still shaky : Conflicting demands. *TI* 21 Ap'69 6 : 7-8+

Bihar Congress in good shape : Opposition in disarray. *TI* 8 Fe'69 6 : 7-8

Cong(R) sure to fare well in Bihar. *TI* 15 Ja'71 1 : 7-8+

Land reforms tempo quickens in Bihar. *TI* 16 Ag'70 9 : 1-4

Mounting tension in Bihar : Rival demonstrations. *TI* 1 Je'74 4 : 7-8

New alignments in Bihar : Congress infighting. *TI* 18 Fe'75 4 : 7-8

No rice in ration shops in Bihar : Procurement fiasco. *TI* 29 Ja'74 4 : 7-8

Smallpox scourge in Bihar : A belated campaign. *TI* 2 Jl'74 4 : 7-8

Tarkeshwari Sinha faces stiff contest. *TI* 6 Mr'72 5 : 4-5

Two Bhumihars main contenders. *TI* 22 Fe'71 5 : 6-7

A whiff of change : Bihar. *TI (Mag)* 3 Ag'69 1 : 4-6

JOSHI, S.M.

Bihar movement—Objectives and perspective. *Janata* 29(41) 17 Nv-24 Nv'74 5-6+

Light versus darkness. *Janata* 29(28) 15 Ag'74 5-8

JUTE industry and trade

Marketing of jute in Madhipura mandi of Saharsa district in Bihar. C.K. Ambastha and B.N. Das *Bihar Inform* 18(19) 16 Nv'70 13-14

KABAD, B.K.R.

The coalition issue : No easy choice for Congress. *TI* 15 Mr'69 6 : 3-5

KANTA PRASAD

Role of commercial banks in development. *Southern Econ* 8(20) 15 Fe'70 21-23

KAPADIA, Alpa

    See Parikh, Sonal jt. auth.

KASHYAP, V.P.

Family planning in Bihar. *Bihar Inform* 18(7) 16 Ap'70 1-2

KENNEDY, Kenneth A.R.

Anatomical description of two crania from Ramgarh : An ancient site in Dhalbhum, Bihar. *J Indian anthrop Soc* 7(2) Oc'72 129-41 tabs fig bibliogr

KHADI industry and trade

Development of Khadi and village industries in Bihar. Siddheshwar Prasad *Khadi Gramodyog* 21(1) Oc'74 21-22

KHAN, Rasheeduddin
   A battle of principles. *Seminar* 75 Nv'65 19-25 bibliogr

KHAN, S.A.
   Growth of food grain production in Bihar. *Indian J agric Econ* 24(2) Ap-Je'69 94-99 tabs ft-n

KHARIA, The
   Kharia birth statistics of Nawatoli. Asesh Kumar Haldar *Vanyajati* 19(2-3) Ap-Jl'71 tabs bibliogr

KHUDA Bakhsh Oriental Public Library, Patna
   Khuda Bakhsh Library contains rare and fabulous manuscripts. *TI* 12 De'69 5 : 1-4

   Khuda Bakhsh Oriental Public Library. *Cultural Forum* 9(2-3) Ja-Ap'67 117-21+

   The Khuda Bakhsh Oriental Public Library. S.N. Sahai *ill Wkly India* 88(38) 22 Oc'67 26-27 ills

KISHORE, V.N.
   Jamshedpur strike : What were the facts. *Janata* 15(5) 22 Fe'70 14

KONAR, Harekrishna
   Bhagalpur session of extended Central Kisan Council. *People's Democracy* 7(1) 3 Ja'71 3+

KRISHNAN, Unni
   Bihar : Front ministry grapples with grim legacy of Congress misrule. *New Age* 15(21) 21 My'67 3+

   Ranadive shows no respect for truth in villifying CPI. *New Age* 15(40) 1 Oc'67 7+

KULKARNI, V.R.
      See Mandal, S.C. jt. auth.

KUMAR, A.
      See Singh, R.P. jt. auth.

KUMAR, N.
   Historical monument of Patna. *Bihar Inform* 18(2) 25 Ja'70 14-16 bibliogr-ft-n

LABOUR and labouring classes
   Aspects of tribal labour force in Chotanagpur. L.P. Vidyarthi *Tribe* 6(3) De'69 54-62
      See also
   Trade unions

LABOUR disputes

Labour unrest. *Link* 8(17) 5 De'65 16-17

Settlement in Bhilai mines. *New Age* 15(28) 9 Jl'67 6

LABOUR laws and legislation

Labour laws are violated in Bihar. *New Age* 15(17) 23 Ap'67 10

LABOUR supply

Labour market in rural Darbhanga. Surendra Prasad Sinha and Modnath Jha *Khadi Gramodyog* 18(6) Mr'72 391-94 tabs

LADEJINSKLY, Wolf

Green revolution in Bihar. *econ and Political Wkly (Suppl)* 43(9) 23 Se'69 A-147-A-62 bibliogr-ft-n

LAKSHMISWAR Public Library, Darbhanga

Darbhanga Library's progress. *TI* 14 Ja'71 3 : 5-6

LAL, Rama Shanker

Dighwara : A urban 'service centre' in the lower Ghaghara-Gandak Doab. *nat Geographical J India* 14(2-3) Je-Se'69 200-13 tabs maps bibliogr-ft-n

The impact of industrialisation in lower Ghaghara Gandak Doab. *Deccan Geographer* 12(2) Jl-De'74 117-26 map

Transport and accessibility in lower Ghaghara Gandak Doab. *Deccan Geographer* 7(1) Ja-Je'69 14-34 tab fig bibliogr

LAL, Sita Ram

*Bihar Control Orders, 1971 as amended upto 31.1.71. Anand Prakash. 1971, 228p. Rs 15

LAND

All set for land struggle : Congressmen cooperate in Bihar. P.S. Madan *New Age* 23(26) 29 Je'75 4

*Bihar survey manual. Srinathprasad Srivastav. Shri Prakash Pub. 1961, iv, 50p. Rs 5

Land use and planning of Nagra. R.P. Singh *Deccan Geographer* 13(1-2) Ja-De'75 165-72 tabs figs

"Sathi" land scandal. *Link* 5(50) 21 Jl'63 12

———— : Mathematical models

Experimental land utilisation surveys in cadastrally unsur-veyed areas through direct plot to plot observations, Bihar 1956-57. J.M. Sengupta and others *Sankhya (B)* 26(1-2) Nv'64 69-88 tabs

Giridih : Its growth and land use. K. Bagchi and U. Sen *Geographical Rev India* 25(4) De'63 243-50

LAND laws and legislation

Land legislation must be strictly enforced in Bihar. K.B. Sahay *Political and econ Rev* 1(27) 7 Se'70 7

LAND reforms

Ban on sale of farm land in Bihar. A.K. Sen *Swarajya* 15(43) 24 Ap'71 12

Bataidari reforms. *Weekend Rev* 2(27) 8 Je'68 20

Bihar at last moves on land question : Faces centre's obstruction on Tata zamindari—Willing to curb urban property holdings. *Link* 14(37) 23 Ap'72 20-21

Bihar ceilings; editorial. *TI* 5 Ag'71 6 : 2

Bihar ceilings; editorial. *TI* 1 Ja'72 8 : 1-2

Bihar Govt. approves ceiling ordinances.   *TI* 31 Jl'71 1 : 2-5

Bihar : Kulak lobby in action. K. Gopalan   *New Age* 20(20) 14 My'72 16

Bihar land reforms—A sour joke : Verdict of the working group on land reforms. *New Age* 21(19) 13 My'73 4-5

*Bihar land reforms (fixation of ceiling and acquisition of surplus land), rules, 1963. Malhotra, C.P. 1964, 83p. Rs 2.50

Bihar ordinance ready to limit property holdings. K. Gopalan *New Age* 19(32) 8 Ag'71 3

Bihar : United meet on surplus land. P.S. Madan *New Age* 23(27) 6 Jl'75 6

Bihar's rural poor in bitter confrontation with landlords. Prabhat Dasgupta *New Age* 22(44) 3 Nv'74 3+

CPI to move for lowering Bihar land ceiling. *New Age* 19(21) 23 My'71 13

Congressmen join Bihar surplus land convention. P.S. Madan *New Age* 23(25) 22 Je'75 5

Controversy over Tata zamindari. *TI* 23 Je'70 11 : 1-3

Half-backed reform; editorial. *TI* 15 Se'70 8 : 2

Jamshedpur's future : New climate of uncertainty. Sankar Ghosh *TI* 9 Jl'70 6 : 3-5+

Land ceiling Act, 1961. Thakur Prasad *Organiser* 21(13) 5 Nv'67 7

Land reform in Bihar—The issues involved. *New Age*
20(29)   16 Jl'72   4

Land reforms only solution, says CPI. *New Age* 23(24)
15 Je'75   3

Land reforms tempo quickens in Bihar. Jitendra Singh *TI*
16 Ag'70   9 : 1-4

Landlords block ceiling implementation in Bihar. P.S.
Madan *New Age* 23(30)   27 Jl'75   11 ·

New crisis in Bihar Govt's land policy. Indradeep Sinha
New Age 10(27)   8 Jl'62   7+

Pioneering measures. *Link* 13(52)   8 Ag'71   20-21

A question of principles in Bihar. *Link* 14(16)   28 Nv'71
21-22

Strong vested interests active in Bihar. *TI*   30 Oc'72
1 : 1-5+

Tata zamindari goes : New bill passed in Bihar Assembly.
K. Gopalan *New Age* 20(26)   25 Je'72   7

'Vigorous implementation', Mishra style in Bihar. *New Age*
23(25)   22 Je'75   6

LAND revenue

Another fiasco. *Link* 8(19)   19 De'65   17-18

Bihar also prepares against land revenue enhancement.
New Age 10(37)   16 Se'62   1+

Land revenue abolition—A point of view with reference
to Bihar. *Southern Econ* 10(11)   1 Oc'71   13-14

_____ : History

History of land revenue of Chota-Nagpur in the first half
of the 19th century. J.C. Jha *J Bihar Res Soc*   50(1-4)
Ja-De'64   105-13

LAND settlement

Functional classification of urban settlement in Singbhum
district, Bihar : A cartographical appraisal. Tridib Kumar
Basu *Geographical Rev India* 37(2) Je'75   165-71 tabs
bibliogr appdx

LAND tenure

Abolition of Tata zamindari. Jagannath Sarkar *Mainstream*
8(44)   4 Jl'70   19-22

Assent to Bill on abolition of Tata zamindari withheld.
Swaminathan S. Aiyar *TI* 26 Oc'71   1 : 7-8+

Bihar UF Govt. to protect tenants. K. Gopalan *New Age* 15(42) 15 Oc'67 7

Tata zamindari must go. Jagannath Sarkar *New Age* 19(46) 14 Nv'71 6; 19(47) 21 Nv'71 6

Tata zamindari to go. K. Gopalan *New Age* 15(34) 20 Ag'67 4

Tata's zamindari. *Link* 9(50) 23 Jl'67 17-18

*Tenancy restriction on protected tenants. Srinathprasad Srivastav. Rung Bahadur Singh. 1962, iv, 35p. 22cm. Rs 3

Tenants on Tata zamindari being thrown out. *New Age* 11(50) 15 De'63 6

Tenurial reform in Bihar. Sailesh Kumar Bose *econ Stud* 4(6) De'63 291-96+

_____ : History

Bihar tenantry (1783-1833). Ram Narain Sinha. People's Pub H. 1968, xii, 190p. Rs 20 Review
Indian econ soc Hist Rev 8(4) De'71 463-65; *Indica* 8(2) Se'71 122-24

_____ : Law

Attack on share-croppers. *Link* 10(12) 29 Oc'67 19

BJS opposes Communist tampering with Bihar Land Ceiling Act, 1961. Thakur Prasad *Organiser* 21(13) 5 Nv'67 7

Share-croppers in Bihar. *Commerce* 115(2948) 11 Nv'67 1122-23

LANGUAGE problem
Bihar consensus on language. *Link* 11(2) 25 Ag'68 22

Why Urdu cannot, and shall not be the second language of Bihar. *Organiser* 20(50) 30 Jl'67 5

LEGISLATORS
Political elite in Bihar. Shashi Shanker Jha. Vora. 1972, 332p. Rs 25 Review
Commerce 125(3212) 25 Nv'72 1347

LEGISLATURE : Legislative Assembly
Election results at a glance-4. *Yojana* 11(9) 14 My'67 16

Two-pronged attack on Sahay. *Link* 7(35) 11 Ap'65 13

_____ : Legislative Council
Upper houses : Congress dilemma. *Mainstream* 8(35) 2 My'70 9-10

Vidhan Parishad abolition. *Link* 12(36) 19 Ap'70 10

LEUVA, K.K.

*The Asur, a study of primitive iron-smelters. Bharatiya adimjati sevak sangh. 1963, xviii, 234p. pls bibliogr 22.5cm. Rs 17.50

LIBRARIES

Library movement in Bihar. Jogesh Misra *Herald Libr Sci* 3(2-3) Ap-Jl'64 185-93 bibliogr

    See also

Khuda Bakhsh Oriental Public Library, Patna

LICENSES

Shady deals. *Link* 9(42) 28 My'67 21-22

LIMAYE, Madhu

The Bihar movement : Some questions. *Janata* 29(23) 14 Jl'74 4-6

LOCAL government

Civic administration of cantonments in Bihar. Nawal Kishore Prasad Verma *quart J Local Self-Government Inst* 35(2) Oc-De'65 185-94

LOOMBA, Satish

Big business mounts offensive, factional feuds beset INTUC. *New Age* 13(8) 21 Fe'65 5

Security guards, police attack Bhilai Workers. *New Age* 15(28) 9 Jl'67 6

MADAN, P.S.

All set for land struggle : Congressmen cooperative in Bihar. *New Age* 23(26) 29 Je'75 4

Bihar CPI supports post-emergency steps. *New Age* 23(31) 3 Ag'75 12

Bihar : Mishra starts with big goodwill. *New Age* 23(20) 18 My'75 11

Bihar : United meet on surplus land. *New Age* 23(27) 6 Jl'75 6

Congressmen join Bihar surplus land convention. *New Age* 23(25) 22 Je'75 5

Landlords block ceiling implementation in Bihar. *New Age* 23(30) 27 Jl'75 11

MAHARATHI, U.

Arts and crafts. *ill Wkly India* 89(12) 24 Mr'68 40-41

MAHATI, Mohanlal (Viyogi)
*Bihar. Rajhans. 1960, 46p. Rs 1.75

MAHATO, Pashupati Prasad
Around the koel and Kanhar. *Folklore* 8(7) Jl'67 238-43

Impact of Brahminical culture on the tribes of Chotanagpur : IND festival—A case study. *Folklore* 13(11) Nv'72
452·60 bibliogr

MAHILIS, The
The Mahilis. P.C. Roy Choudhry *mod Rev* 116(6) De'64
466-70 bibliogr

MAHMOOD, A. and Ram Kumar
"A bumper harvest from wheat" in Bihar. *Bihar Inform*
17(20) 1 De'69 25+

MAHTO, Satya Narayan
Organisation of trade in the rural area of Ranchi district.
Bull Cult Res Inst 10(1-2) 1974 86-91 bibliogr

MAIZE
Maize seed production in Bihar : Rameshwar Singh *Bihar
Inform* 18(11) 16 Je'70 5-8 tabs appdx

MAJI, C.C.
        See Jha, Dayanatha. jt. auth.

MALAVIYA, K.D.
HEC makes progress despite delayed delivery schedules.
Capital 162(4046) 23 Ja'69 143-45

MALHOTRA, Inder
How Harijans suffer : Prejudice and persecution.   *TI*
19 Jl'73 6 : 3-5

MALHOTRA, P.C.
*Social economic survey of Bihar city and Bairagarh. Asia.
1964, 235p. Rs 25

MANDAL, B.B.
Acceptability and awareness of family planning. *Voluntary
Action* 16(6) Nv-De'74 29-31 bibliogr

Caste and occupational mobility in two industrial towns of
Bihar. *J soc Res* 16(1) Mr'73 59-64 tabs bibliogr-
ft-n

MANDAL, Bishweshwar
Manufacturing regions of North Bihar. *nat Geographical J
India* 17(1) Mr'71 51-62 bibliogr-ft-n

MANDAL, S.C. and Kulkarni, V.R.

Scope for expansion of high-yielding varieties in Bihar. *Indian Fmg* 21(7) Oc'71 104-05 tab

———— and Sinha, M.P.

Soil fertility and fertilizer problems in Bihar. *Indian Fmg* 21(1) Ap'71 5-6+

MANPOWER

Manpower-utilisation in East Bihar villages. C.K. Ambastha and N.K. Jaiswal *Rural India* 32(11) Nv'69 273-75 tab

> *See also*

Labour supply

MARKETING, Co-operative

Agricultural marketing co-operatives. *Bihar Inform* 16(16) 16 Se'68 5

Bihar State Co-operative Marketing Union. *Commerce (Suppl)* 127(3263) 17 Nv'73 76

Co-operative marketing of agricultural produce makes headway. *Bihar Inform* 16(20) 1 De'68 14

MARKETS

Culture change in an intertribal market. D.P. Sinha. Asia. 1968, 112p. Rs 25 Review
Eastern Anthropologist 22(1) Ja-Ap'69 132-33; *econ and Political Wkly* 4(21) 24 My'69 873-77; *Man in India* 50(4) Oc-De'70 425-26

Grain markets for Bihar held up land acquisition hurdle. Jitendra Singh *TI* 15 Jl'75 4 : 7-8

The Phariya in an intertribal market. D.P. Sinha *econ and Political Wkly* 2(31) 5 Ag'67 1373-78 bibliogr-ft-n

MARKETS, Rural

Organisation of trade in the rural area of Ranchi district. Satya Narayan Mahto *Bull Cult Res Inst* 10(1-2) 1974 86-91 bibliogr

MARRIAGE

Effect of changes in age-patterns of marriage on fertility rates in Bihar, 1961-86. Shailendra Nath Banerjee *Man in India* 53(3) Jl-Se'73 262-78 tabs bibliogr

MARRIAGE customs and rites

The ways of acquiring mates in tribal Chotanagpur. B.N. Ghosh *Folklore* 8(11) Nv'67 403-10 bibliogr

MATHUR, B.L. and Srivastava, G.P.L.
  Some aspects of the Bihar mass vasectomy camps. *J Family Welfare* 20(3) Mr'74 73-83 tabs bibliogr

MATHUR, J.C.
  Historical-cultural heritage. *Marg* 20(1) De'66 4-12 ills

MEDICAL care
  Doctor's ailment. *Link* 6(27) 16 Fe'64 12
  Doctors discuss health. *Link* 8(4) 5 Se'65 20-21
  Health services in Bihar. *Bihar Inform* 16(20) 1 De'68 8-11

MEDICAL colleges
  Medical colleges or teaching shops? N.K. Singh *econ and Political Wkly* 7(19) 6 My'72 920

MEHDI, S G. and Sinha, J.N.
  A study of relationship between neuroticism and job satisfaction in school teachers. *Indian J appl Psychol* 8(1) Ja'71 46-47 bibliogr-ft-n

MEHTA, Surendra Sen
  Bihar records all-round progress. *Yojana* 17(9) 1 Je'73 379-80

MINERS
  Bihar miners serve bonus strike notice. K. Gopalan *New Age* 14(13) 27 Mr'66 6

MINES and mineral resources
  Mineral and mining resources. B.B. Engineer *ill Wkly India* 89(12) 24 Mr'68 30-33

_____ : History
  Development of the mineral industries of Bihar : 1833-1918. Pabitra Bhaskar Sinha *J Historical Res* 16(1) Ag'73 74-86 ft-n

MISHRA, Chandra Mohan
  A confusing picture. *Link* 16(25) 26 Ja'74 37-38

MISHRA, D.R.
  Experiences in seed production in Bihar. *Bihar Inform* 18(7) 16 Ap'70 3-4

MISHRA, Girish
  Agricultural labour in Bihar. *mod Rev* 118(4) Oc'65 312-20
  Bihar mosaic. *Mainstream* 9(25) 20 Fe'71 11+

Challenge and opportunity. *Mainstream* 10(30) 25 Mr'72 10-12

Devious ways of reactionary combine. *Mainstream* 10(27) 4 Mr'72 9-10+

Indigo plantation and the agrarian relations in Champaran during the nineteenth century. *Indian econ soc Hist Rev* 3(4) De'66 332-57 bibliogr

Socio-economic background of Gandhi's Champaran Movement. *Indian econ soc Hist Rev* 5(3) Se'68 245-76 bibliogr-ft-n

Where Daroga Rai tripped. *Mainstream* 9(17) 26 De'70 12+

——— and Pandey, Braj Kumar

Bihar : Fall of Paswan Ministry. *Mainstream* 6(45) 6 Jl'68 31-32

Bihar in the cesspool of instability. *Mainstream* 7(30) 29 Mr'69 11-12+

Bihar teachers' strike and after. *Mainstream* 7(35) 3 My'69 34-35

Bihar's political fish-market. *Mainstream* 7(43) 28 Je'69 8-10+

Bihar's second UF Government. *Mainstream* 6(44) 29 Je'68 15-16

C.R. Pant rules Bihar! *Mainstream* 7(41) 14 Je'69 24-27

Instability continues. *Mainstream* 7(25) 22 Fe'69 9-10+

Reaction's all-round retreat. *Mainstream* 9(30) 27 Mr'71 17-20

United Front balance sheet. *Mainstream* 6(24) 10 Fe'68 8-11

MISHRA, J.N.

J.N. Mishra elected unanimously. *TI* 7 Ag'75 1 : 5-6+

MISHRA, Jagannath

Making up the gap in power supply. *Commerce (Suppl)* 127(3263) 17 Nv'73 23-24

MISHRA, Madaneshwar

Changing agrarian economy of Purnea district : 1765-1950. *J Bihar Res Soc* 58(1-4) Ja-De'72 197-223 tabs bibliogr-ft-n

MISRA, B.R., *ed.*

*Report on socio-economic survey of Jamshedpur city. Patna Univ. 1959, Rs 10

MISRA, Govind

> History of Bihar (1740-1772). Munshiram. 187p. Rs 22
> Review
> *TI* 1 Ag'71 10 : 5-6

MISRA, Jogesh

> Library movement in Bihar. *Herald Libr Sci* 3(2-3) Ap-Jl'64
> 185-93 bibliogr

MISRA, Ram Niwas

> Growth of population in the lower Ganga-Ghaghra Doab.
> *Indian Geographical J* 45(1-2)   Ja-Mr & Ap-Je'70   27-32
> figs bibliogr

MITHILA

> Domestic arts of Mithila. J.C. Mathur and Mildred Archer
> *Marg* 20(1) De'66 43-52 ills

MOHAMMED OMAIR ALAM

> Profile of progressive farmer. *Kurukshetra* 20(14) 16 Ap'72
> 14-15

MOHAMMEDANS in Bihar

> A battle of principles. Rasheeduddin Khan *Seminar* 75
> Nv'65 19-25 bibliogr

> GOI's U.P.—Bihar Muslim officers inject communal poison
> in Kashmir : Five serious cases. Mohammed Abdullah
> Kashmiri *Organiser* 19(8) 3 Oc'65 8-9

> Three lakh Bihari Muslim families have members in
> Pakistan. *Organiser* 18(39) 10 My'65 16

MONASTERIES, Buddhist

> Vikramasila monastery—An ancient seat of learning.
> Dipak Kumar Barua *Maha Bodhi* 75(5-6) My-Je'67 204-05

MORTGAGE banks

> Bihar state co-operative land mortgage bank and supply of
> credit. M.M. Prasad *Indian J Commerce* 21(2) Je'68
> 31-39

MOTE, A.P.

> A flood of memories. *TI* 28 Se'75 9 : 1-4

MUHAMMAD Fahim-ud-Din

> *Animal production in Bihar. Asia. 1963, xii, 166p. tabs
> bibliogr 24.5cm. Rs 18.50

MUKERJEE, Dilip

> Bihar's crumbling parties : The dynamics of disintegration.
> *TI* 27 Fe'71 6 : 3-5+

Hard fight ahead of new Congress in Bihar. *TI* 28 Fe'71
1 : 2-4+

MUKERJI, S.K.

Bihar ushers in Rajendra Agricultural University. *Indian Fmg* 20(11) Fe'71 33-36

MUKHERJEE, Parimal

'*Garibi hatao andolan*' in Bihar. *Yojana* 17(5) 1 Ap'73 225-27

MUKHERJEE, Sadhan

Bihar Communist Party will register big advance. *New Age* 17(6) 9 Fe'69 4+

CPI Kedar's will win Jamshedpur seat. *New Age* 19(10) 7 Mr'71 12

CPI-35, Congress-167, PSP-4 : Big victory of Bihar electoral entente. *New Age* 20(12) 19 Mr'72 7

Changing colours of Congress-R candidate. *New Age* 19(8) 21 Fe'71 4

MUKHERJI, Mahamaya

Function and functional classification of towns in Bihar. *Deccan Geographer* 8(1-2) Ja-De'70 56-66 tabs maps bibliogr-ft-n

Need for functional classification of towns. *Patna Univ J* 23(1) Ja'68 60-70 bibliogr-ft-n

Transport towns of Bihar. *Indian Geographical J* 44(3-4) Jl-Oc'69 42-51 tabs maps

MUNDAS, The

The Mundas and their country. Sarat Chandra Roy. Asia. 1970, 407p. Rs 40 Review
Indian Librarian 25(4) Mr'71 225

Murder among the Mundas : A case study. A.B. Saran *Indian J soc Wk* 23(1) Ap'62 1-7

NAMBIAR, K.R.N.

Constitution of India, articles 7 and 5—Migration and domicile—Minor can migrate independently—Article 7 over-rides article-5. *Indian J int Law* 7(4) Oc'67 553-56

NAMBOODIRIPAD, E.M.S.

The Bihar and Kerala struggles. *People's Democracy* 11(2) 12 Ja'75 5+

NANDI, Karuna K.

The D.V.C. and Bihar. *mod Rev* 113(3) Mr'63 182-83

NATIONAL income

Bihar's state income and industrialisation. Subhash Chandra Sarkar *mod Rev* 127(3) Se'70 179-84 tabs bibliogr-ft-n

NATURAL resources

Bihar : A mineral treasury. *Commerce (Annual Number)* 121(3113) 1970 148-49 map

NAXALITES

Face to face. Jayaprakash Narayan *Khadi Gramodyog* 17(3) De'70 201-08

Kill them and call them; editorial. *econ and Political Wkly* 10(23) 7 Je'75 872

Murder to landlords' order. Arvind Narayan Das *econ and Political Wkly* 10(24) 14 Je'75 915-17

Naxalite bogey raised to suppress Harijan resistance to landlords. *People's Democracy* 11(24) 15 De'75 3+

The Naxalite bogey. *Link* 17(42) 1 Je'75 16-18

Polit Bureau condemns brutal killings in Bihar. *People's Democracy* 11(24) 15 De'75 1+

Under the pretext of fighting Naxalite—Open collusion between administration and landlords. Jayaprakash Narayan *Janata* 30(17) 1 Je'75 2+

Wanton killing by police in name of 'Naxalite encounter'. *New Age* 23(24) 15 Je'75 1+

Why a radical revolution; editorial. *Thought* 27(24) 14 Je'75 6+

NEWSPAPERS

> *See also*

Press

_____ : History

Early printing presses and newspapers in Bihar. Jata Shankar Jha *J Bihar Res Soc* 50(1-4) Ja-De'64 98-104

OCCUPATIONS

Caste and occupation in a village in Bihar. K.N. Sahay *Man in India* 47(3) Jl-Se'67 178-88 bibliogr-ft-n

Caste and occupational mobility in two industrial towns of Bihar. B.B. Mandal *J soc Res* 16(1) Mr'73 59-64 tabs bibliogr

Caste and occupational preference in East Bihar villages. N.K. Jaiswal and C.K. Ambastha *Indian J soc Wk* 31(2) Jl'70 191-95 tabs

80 BIHAR

OFFICIALS and employees

Bihar Govt. employees to strike from July 11, 1968. *People's Democracy* 4(27) 7 Jl'68 9

Bihar : Government employees' victory. *People's Democracy* 7(31) 1 Ag'71 7

Bihar NGO leader victimised, ban on processions imposed. K. Gopalan *New Age* 13(12) 21 Mr'65 9

Bihar NGO strike is withdrawn. K. Gopalan *New Age* 16(31) 4 Ag'68 7

Bihar : Unrest among government employees. *Link* 7(25) 31 Ja'65 20

Word and action. *Link* 6(28) 23 Fe'64 18-19

_____ : Salaries, allowances, etc.

Bihar NGO struggle enters new stage. K. Gopalan *New Age* 13(10) 7 Mr'65 9

Fantastic concept of pay structure : Bihar Committee's findings. *New Age* 12(32) 9 Ag'64 17

Govt. employees' demand. *Link* 7(9) 11 Oc'64 15-17

New pay scale fail to meet NGO's demand. K. Gopalan *New Age* 13(27) 4 Jl'65 6

Pay Committee's fantastic wisdom : Bihar govt. employees plan to fight back retrograde Report. Ratan Roy *New Age* 12(44) 1 Nv'64 15

OJHA, B.N.

The saga of electricity in Bihar. *Commerce (Suppl)* 127(3263) 17 Nv'73 59-61

OJHA, Gyaneshwar

Change in the pattern of capital formation in agriculture; summary. *Indian J agric Econ* 24(4) Oc-De'69 138-39

OPIUM industry and trade : History

Ramchand Pandit's Report on opium cultivation in 18th century Bihar. Suprakash Sanyal *Bengal Past & Present* 87(2) Jl-De'68 181-89 bibliogr-ft-n

PADGAONKAR, Dileep

Smallpox scourge in Bihar : A story of prolonged neglect. *TI* 8 Jl'74 4 : 3-5

PAHARIYAS, The

Pahariyas and their customs. B.N. Sahay *Vanyajati* 14(1) Ja'66 7-18 ft-n

PAINTING

Bazaar style.   Mildred Archer *Marg* 20(1) De'66   53-54

PANCHAYATS

*The Bihar gram *cutcherry* rules-1962 (with short notes and comments).   Srinath Prasad Srivastav.   Rung Bahadur Singh.   1962, iv, 40p. 22cm. Rs 2

*The Bihar Panchayat Raj (amendment and validating) Act, 1961 (Bihar Act viii of 1962); supplement to the spot-light on the Bihar Panchayat Raj Act, 1947. Srinath Prasad Srivastav. Rung Bahadur Singh. 1962, ii, 22p. 22cm.

Democracy and development : The grass-roots experience in India. R.C. Prasad. Rachna. 1971, 336p. Review *Indian J Publ Adm* 20(4) Oc-De'74   384-86

"Democracy in action in the villages of Bihar, Orissa and West Bengal." A.B. Datta *quart J Local Self-Government Inst* 36(1) Jl-Se'65   97-103

Panchayati raj in Bihar : A psychic appraisal. Hartiruth Singh *Kurukshetra* 12(3) De'63   14-16

Panchayati raj. *Kurukshetra* 12(1) 2 Oc'63   64

Panchayati raj. *Kurukshetra* 13(1) 2 Oc'64   59

Panchayats in Bihar : A critical study.   B.S. Bhargava *mod Rev* 120(2) Ag'66 140-47   bibliogr-ft-n

People's perception of village panchayat under panchayati raj.   N.K. Jaiswal and K.N.K. Chouhan   *quart J Local Self-Government* 41(3) Ja-Mr'71   267-73

Political consciousness among the tribals and their represent-ation in gram Panchayats. B.N Sahay and B.K. Singh *Vanyajati* 18(1) Ja'70   12-16   tabs

Reorganising panchayats raj in Bihar : A critique of the reform proposals. Haridwar Rai and Awadhesh Prasad *Indian J Publ Adm* 21(1) Ja-Mr'75   19-47   ft-n

*Sarapanca ka adhikar aur kartavya. Revatiramanprasad Simha. Pahuja Bros. (H). 1951, ii, 56p. 22cm. Rs 1.25

*Spot-light on the Bihar Panchayat Raj Act 1947 (Bihar Act xxi of 1959); comments, comparative study and latest case laws up to Dec. 1, 1960. Srinath Prasad Srivastav. Shri Prakash Pub. 1960, xii, 163p. 24.5cm. Rs 10

Study in social participation of elected leaders. R.N.P. Singh and B.P. Singh *quart J Local Self-Government* 43(3) Ja-Mr'73 135-41   tabs

"Three tier panchayat system of Santhals." L.B. Prasad *Vanyajati* 20(1) Ja'72   46-49

PANDEY, Braj Kumar
　　See Mishra, Girish jt. auth.

PANDEY, J. and Sinha, J.B.P.
　Dependence proneness and perceived problems of adjust-ment. *J Psychol Res* 12(3) Se'68 104-10

PANDEY, Kedar
　Industrialisation of Bihar. *Bihar Inform* 18(10) 1 Je'70 1-2

PANDEY, M.P.
　Agriculture in Bihar : Growth rate in rice production has not kept pace with other cereals and pulses. *Yojana* 19(10) 15 Je'75 35-36

　Regional planning in Bihar. *Eastern Econ* 63(6) 9 Ag'74 243-47 tabs

PARAKAL, Pauly V.
　The face of hunger in Bihar. *New Age* 14(48) 27 Nv'66 8-10; 14(49) 4 De'66 8-9

　Harihar mirrors Congress rot. *New Age* 17(9) 2 Mr'69 2

PARIKH, Sonal and Kapadia, Alpa
　Bihar and Bombay students. *Janata* 29(28) 15 Ag'74 39-40

PATALIPUTRA
　Pataliputra. Laksmanprasad Bhardvaj and Yashpal Jain, eds. Sasta Sahitya Mandal. 1959, 30p. 18cm. Re 0.37

PATNA : Floods
　All major rivers rising again : Patna is threatened with new deluge. *TI* 9 Se'75 1 : 1-3

　Army, IAF battle to save Patna. *TI* 27 Ag'75 1 : 1-3+

　Army jawans alerted in Patna. *TI* 10 Se'75 1 : 4+

　Deluge in Patna. *Link* 10(8) 1 Oc'67 17+

　Flood waters invade fresh areas in Eastern Patna. *TI* 29 Ag'75 1 : 1-2

　Flood waters start receding in Patna. *TI* 28 Ag'75 1 : 1-3

　Massive Patna bid to pump out flood water. *TI* 7 Se'75 1 : 7-8

　Patna after the deluge : A trail of misery and destruction. S. Dharmarajan *TI* 22 Se'75 4 : 3-5; 23 Se'75 4 : 7-8

　Patna citizen's ordeal by water. Jitendra Singh *TI* 30 Ag'75 7 : 1-4

Patna floods; letter to the editor. *TI* 4 Se'75   4 : 6

Patna is limping back to life. *TI* 30 Ag'75   1 : 7-8+

Patna may yet be spared the catastrophe of another flood.
TI 12 Se'75   1 : 1-2+

Patna still reeling under flood impact. *TI*   31 Ag'75
1 : 3-4+

Patna's plight; editorial. *TI* 28 Ag'75   4 : 1

People fleeing Patna for fear of epidemics. *TI* 2 Se'75
1 : 1-2+

Two-thirds of Patna still submerged : Half a million
continue to live on rooftops. *TI* 1 Se'75   1 : 1-2+

Unprecedented deluge in Patna : Most city areas under
10 ft. water. *TI* 26 Ag'75   1 : 1-3+

_____ : History

Afghan usurpation of Patna. Govind Mishra   *J Indian Hist*
44(2) Ag'66   545-52   bibliogr-ft-n

_____ : Monuments

Historical monument of Patna. N. Kumar   *Bihar Inform*
18(2)   25 Ja'70   14-16   bibliogr-ft-n

PATNA College, Patna

A history of the Patna college (1863-1963). J.N. Sarkar and
J.C. Jha. 1963, i-iv, 170p. Patna College. Review
J Asiatic Soc (Bengal) 7(1-2)   1965   107

PATNA University

Governors' functions as the Chancellor of the Universities : A case study in Bihar during the period 1952-60.
Naval Kishore Sinha   *Indian J Pol Sci*   23(1)   Ja-Mr'62
72-82   bibliogr-ft-n

Patna University on verge of financial bankruptcy. *TI*
18 De'69   1 : 7-8+

PATRA, Atulcandra

*The administration of justice under the East-India Com-
pany in Bengal, Bihar and Orissa. Asia. 1962, viii, 233p.
21.5cm. Rs 10

PEASANT uprisings

Agrarian unrest and economic change in rural Bihar :
Three case studies. Pradhan H. Prasad   *econ and Political
Wkly* 10(24)   14 Je'75   931-37   tabs ft-n

All support to Bihar peasant struggles. Harekrishna Konar
People's Democracy 4(26)   30 Je'68   2

Bihar Khet Mazdoor Sabha plans agitation. K. Gopalan *New Age* 13(24) 13 Je'65 6

Bihar peasants fight back govt. onslaughts. Bhogendra Jha *New Age* 12(4) 26 Ja'64 16

Bihar's rural poor in bitter confrontation with landlords. Prabhat Dasgupta *New Age* 22(44) 3 Nv'74 3+

Champaran peasants' growing struggle : A serious challenge to Bihar U.F. Government. S.S. Srivastava *People's Democracy* 4(25) 23 Je'68 5+

PEASANTRY

Bhagalpur session of extended Central Kisan Council. Harekrishna Konar *People's Democracy* 7(1) 3 Ja'71 3+

PETECH, Luciano

Mithila and Nepal. *J Bihar Res Soc (Sec III)* Ja-De'62 13-18 bibliogr

PHARMACEUTICAL industry and trade

On developing pharmaceutical industry. D.P. Sharma *Commerce (Suppl)* 127(3263) 17 Nv'73 25-27

POLITICAL parties

Socialism and non-congressism. M.K. Biswas *Janata* 23(46) 15 De'68 4

POLITICS and government : 1962-1966

Anti-Sahay campaign. *Link* 9(16) 27 Nv'66 18

Bihar's bane—Caste. *Link (Annual Number)* 9(1) 15 Ag'66 38

Caste canvas. *Link* 9(18) 11 De'66 18-19

Castism and wastage. *Link* 6(10) 29 Oc'63 20

Chief Minister poisoning stunt. *Organiser* 16(37) 22 Ap'63 4

Conflict over list. *Link* 9(18) 11 De'66 19-20

The Congress band wagon. *Link* 7(6) 20 Se'64 19-20

Demonstration. *Link* 6(36) 19 Ap'64 14-15

Embarrassed members. *Link* 7(30) 7 Mr'65 19-20

Factional politics again. *Link* 5(30) 3 Mr'63 19

Groups and vested interests. *Link* 8(47) 3 Jl'66 15-17

Growing unity against Right reaction. Ali Ashraf *New Age* 11(5) 3 Fe'63 4+

Jha : Caste carriers falling. *Link* 6(1) 15 Ag'63 41

Joint front against Sahay clique : New development in Bihar political scene. Yogindra Sharma *New Age* 13(51) 19 De'65 14

Kamaraj-Kamakhya deal. *Organiser* 18(7) 28 Se'64 13

National policies. *New Age* 10(51) 23 De'62 6

The needs Jharkhand Party to break his chief rival K.B. Sahay of Chota Nagpur. *Organiser* 16(45) 24 Je'63 5

New era in Congress? *Link* 7(50) 25 Jl'65 15-17

Open struggle to topple Jha Ministry. Ali Ashraf *New Age* 11(13) 31 Mr'63 6

Raja Bahadur in Congress. *Link* 8(42) 29 My'66 11-13

Revolt in Bihar. *Link* 6(38) 3 My'64 11

Rivals are warming up. *Link* 8(31) 13 Mr'66 11

Sahay insists using DIR against opposition parties. K. Gopalan *New Age* 14(14) 3 Ap'66 5

Sahay Ministry indicted : Debate on no-confidence motion. K. Gopalan *New Age* 12(34) 23 Ag'64 2

Sahay's inhibitions. *Link* 8(8) 3 Oc'65 21-22

Setback to dissidents. *Link* 9(4) 4 Se'66 17

Some aspects of Bihar politics. Chetakar Jha and Shree Nagesh Jha *India quart* 20(3) Jl-Se'64 312-29 tabs bibliogr-ft-n

Swatantra entry upsets Congress power balance. K. Gopalan *New Age* 12(39) 27 Se'64 7

Tarnished. *Link* 7(2) 23 Ag'64 18

The tussle begins. *Link* 6(18) 15 De'63 17-18

Uncertainty. *Link* 6(3) 1 Se'63 18-19

Vitiated atmosphere in group policies. Ali Ashraf *New Age* 11(14) 7 Ap'63 6

———— : 1967

After West Bengal, Bihar? *Link* 10(18) 10 De'67 14-16

Ambiguity in Constitution needs to be cleared. Jayaprakash Narayan *Voluntary Action* 2(6) Nv-De'67 3-5

Anti-climax to toppling drama. K. Gopalan *New Age* 15(39) 24 Se'67 4

Ayyangar forced to retire for not dismissing UF Govt. K. Gopalan *New Age* 15(50) 10 De'67 16+

Bihar Coalition adopts 33-point programme; text of programme adopted by the parties in the Coalition Government. *Organiser* 20(31) 19 Mr'67 7

Bihar Congress hatching plot against UF. Govt. K. Gopalan *New Age* 15(16) 16 Ap'67 3+

Bihar : Creditable record. *Link* 10(2) 20 Ag'67 19-20

The Bihar crisis. *Link* 10(4) 3 Se'67 14-16

Bihar defection bomb proves a damp squib. *New Age* 15(36) 3 Se'67 1

Bihar : Frozen crisis. *Link* 10(5) 10 Se'67 15-16

Bihar Jana Sangh flouting agreed programme. *New Age* 15(40) 1 Oc'67 16

Bihar. Ramashray Roy *Seminar* 95 Jl'67 35-41 tabs

Bihar UF alerts people about Bengal-model coup. K. Gopalan *New Age* 15(50) 10 De'67 4

Bihar's first non-Congress ministry. *Link* 9(31) 12 Mr'67 12-14

Bihar's murky politics. A.K. Sen *Swarajya* 12(13) 23 Se'67 9-10

Birth of a Coalition. *Link* 9(30) 5 Mr'67 21-22

Coalition farce. *Link* 10(7) 24 Se'67 11-14

Coalition Government must survive. Jagannath Sarkar *New Age* 15(34) 20 Ag'67 3

Coalition stays. *Link* 9(48) 9 Jl'67 13

Congress-Mandal claim in Bihar is ridiculous. *Organiser* 21(4) 3 Se'67 15

Congress plots for central intervention in Bihar. K. Gopalan *New Age* 15(25) 18 Je'67 16+

Dis-united Front. *Link* 10(20) 24 De'67 11-12

End gangster regime. *New Age* 15(3) 15 Ja'67 2

First BJS Ministers. *Organiser* 20(30) 12 Mr'67 16+

Jana Sangh out to create trouble in Bihar. *New Age* 15(51) 17 De'67 11

Need for pragmatic policies in Bihar. *Eastern Econ* 48(11) 17 Mr'67 437

Non-Congress ministry takes office in Bihar. *New Age* 15(11) 12 Mr'67 5

People's victory in Bihar-Congress plot smashed. K. Gopalan *New Age* 15(32) 6 Ag'67 16

Plan to topple ministry. *Link* 9(43) 4 Je'67 21

Political kaleidoscope. *Commerce* 115(2942) 30 Se'67 738-39

Problems of implementation. *Link* 9(33) 26 Mr'67 22-23

Programme of the non-Congress government (Documents). *United Asia* 19(2) Mr-Ap'67 133-35

Quit or face no-confidence : Rebel's ultimatum to Bihar Congress bosses. K. Gopalan *New Age* 15(29) 16 Jl'67 12

Sahay's authoritarian regime must end. K. Gopalan *New Age* 15(4) 22 Ja'67 2

Sahay's bid to prevent free poll. K.U. Warier *New Age* 15(7) 12 Fe'67 3

Slow motion politics. *Link* 10(11) 22 Oc'67 20

A sordid affair. *Capital* 159(3977) 7 Se'67 438

Suspense. *Link* 10(21) 31 De'67 19

Trouble in both camps. *Link* 10(14) 12 Nv'67 20

    See also

Bharatiya Kranti Dal : Bihar unit

Elections

Sahay, K.B.

———— : 1968

After the crisis in Bihar; editorial. *Thought* 20(26) 29 Je'68 3-4

Bihar CPI Council on new Coalition Govt. *New Age* 16(16) 21 Ap'68 6

The Bihar conspiracy. *Organiser* 21(26) 4 Fe'68 1+

Bihar conspirators in desperate mood. K. Gopalan *New Age* 16(4) 28 Ja'68 11

The Bihar experience. Indradeep Sinha *Link* 10(25) 26 Ja'68 34-41

Bihar : Fall of Paswan ministry. Girish Mishra and Braj Kumar Pandey *Mainstream* 6(45) 6 Jl'68 31-32

Bihar : Initial steps for Left unity. K. Gopalan *New Age* 16(30) 28 Jl'68 5

Bihar ministry collapse inevitable. K. Gopalan *New Age* 16(9) 3 Mr'68 9

Bihar : Operation topple. *Link* 10(26) 4 Fe'68 10-12

Revisionist opportunism again in Bihar. *People's Democracy* 4(19)   12 My'68   12+

Rise and fall of Bihar ministries. *Commerce* 117(2983) 6 Jl'68   14-15

SSP creates crisis. *Link* 10(36)   14 Ap'68   15-16

Shuffling the pack; editorial. *econ and Political Wkly* 3(12) 23 Mr'68   475-76

Significance of West Bengal. S.A. Dange *Mainstream* 6(21) 20 Ja'68   9-11

United Front balance sheet. Girish Mishra and Braj Kumar Pandey *Mainstream* 6(24)   10 Fe'68   8-11

The way out in Bihar. *Thought* 20(12)   23 Mr'68   4

A welcome development in Bihar; editorial. *Thought* 20(49) 7 De'68   5

   See also

Indian National Congress—Bihar unit

——— : 1969

Ample uncertainty. *Thought* 21(3)   18 Ja'69   7-8

BKD Chief expels four defectors : Bihar ministry list soon. *TI*   3 Mr'69   1 : 4-5

Bhola Paswan fall ascribed to Adivasi politics. Anil Kumar Sinha *Janata* 24(32)   31 Ag'69   7+

Bihar blow. *Link* 12(9)   12 Oc'69   7-8

Bihar C.M. given free hand in cabinet formation. *TI* 2 Mr'69   9 : 4-5

Bihar C.M. to submit list today. *TI*   4 Mr'69   1 : 4+

Bihar Coalition still shaky : Conflicting demands. Jitendra Singh *TI*   21 Ap'69   6 : 7-8+

Bihar Congress Coalition evokes all round contempt. K. Gopalan *New Age* 17(11)   16 Mr'69   7

Bihar : Congress may be allowed to form ministry. *TI* 30 Jl'69   1 : 7-8+

Bihar Congress plans to form post-election coalition. K. Gopalan *New Age* 17(2)   12 Ja'69   7

Bihar Congressmen politicking again. *TI*   16 Fe'69 1 : 2-5+

Bihar Governor asks Bhola Paswan to form new ministry. *TI* 22 Je'69   1 : 7-8+

Bihar ministry quits following defeat in the Vidhan Sabha.
TI 21 Je'69   1 : 1-3+

Bihar placed under President's rule : Assembly suspended.
TI 5 Jl'69   1 : 1-3

Bihar : Political turmoil again.   *Commerce*   118(3034)
28 Je'69   1288

Bihar SVD ministry resigns : Withdrawal of support by
Sangh.   *TI* 2 Jl'69   1 : 6-7+

Bihar scene : The politics of suspended animation. S.K.
Jha *J soc Stud State Govts* 2(3)   Jl-Se'69   171-73

Bihar's ordeal; editorial.   *TI* 23 Je'69   6 : 1

Bihar's political fish-market. Girish Mishra and Braj Kumar
Pandey *Mainstream* 7(43) 28 Je'69   8-10+

Bihar's travail; editorial.   *TI* 21 Nv'69   8 : 2

Caste-based politics of opportunism. L.P. Sinha *Link* 12(1)
15 Ag'69   62-65

Claim by 3-party alliance.   *TI*   24 Fe'69   1 : 3+

The Coalition issue : No easy choice for Congress. B.K.R.
Kabad *TI* 15 Mr'69   6 : 3-5

Congress Board approves Bihar Coalition.   *TI* 28 Fe'69
9 : 5

Congress Coalition may take office today in Bihar amid
protests. *TI* 26 Fe'69   1 : 4-5

Congress leaders do not want Swatantra in Bihar Coalition.
TI 27 Fe'69   4 : 1-2

Congress-led Coalition in Bihar soon.   *TI* 4 Nv'69   1 : 5

Congress may form Govt in Bihar early next month.   *TI*
2 Ag'69   7 : 2-3

Congress, SSP state claim to form cabinet in Bihar.   *TI*
21 Se'69   1 : 1-2+

Congress strategy in Bihar similiar to that of opposition. *TI*
14 Ja'69   5 : 2-4

Contest for leadership likely in Bihar.   *TI* 19 Fe'69 7 : 4-5

Contradictory claims.   *Link*   11(51)   3 Ag'69   15-16

Efforts by P.M. group to form Coalition Government in
Bihar. *TI* 16 De'69   5 : 2-3

Feud in Bihar Congress over spoils of power. K. Gopalan
New Age 17(17)   27 Ap'69   7+

Governor's talk on new Bihar Govt.   *TI* 2 Jl'69   7 : 1-2

Harihar seeks permission to form Coalition in Bihar. *TI* 6 Oc'69 1 : 1-5

Harihar Singh may be asked to resign : Talks in Delhi soon. *TI* 3 Se'69 1 : 7-8

Harihar's efforts. *Link* 11(29) 2 Mr'69   14-15

High Command view on Ramgarh Raja puts C.M. in a fix. *TI* 6 Mr'69 1 : 6-7+

How Congress ministry collapsed in Bihar. *Organiser* 22(46) 28 Je'69 1-2

Ill-advised; editorial. *TI* 8 Jl'69 6 : 1-2

Incredible folly; editorial. *TI* 11 Mr'69 6 : 1-2

Kanungo's decision on Harihar's claim after some time. *TI* 7 Nv'69 1 : 7-8+

Land reform, political stability—Main issues in Bihar poll. *TI* 11 Ja'69 5 : 1-3

Left democratic alternative?   *Link* *(Republic Day Number)* 11(24) 26 Ja'69   22-27

MP's demand popular Govt in Bihar. *TI* 14 De'69 21 : 2-3

Meddling with inquiry. *Link* 11(35) 13 Ap'69 24

Ministry-making. *Link* 11(28) 23 Fe'69 17-18

More horse-trading. *Link* 11(47) 6 Jl'69 13-14

New three-man Bihar ministry's fate may be decided on Wednesday. *TI* 23 Je'69 1 : 1-3

Nijalingappa claims Congress can form Bihar Coalition Govt. *TI* 7 Oc'69 1 : 2-3+

No clear mandate; editorial. *TI* 15 Fe'69 6 : 1-2

Permanent instability. *Thought* 21(52) 27 De'69 9

President's rule; editorial. *TI* 3 Jl'69 6 : 1

President's rule in Bihar from today : Long spell likely. *TI* 4 Jl'69 1 : 6-7+

The Ramgarh episode. *Link* 11(41) 25 My'69 14-15

Revolt if Congress rules. *TI* 23 Fe'69 1 : 4-5

The rumpus about Bihar. *Thought* 20(11) 15 Mr'69 5

SSP member removed from Bihar Vidhan Sabha after a row. *TI* 13 Je'69 5 : 1-2

SSP renews claim to form Govt in Bihar. *TI* 3 De'69 1 : 8+

Swatantra to support Congress Coalitions on certain conditions. *TI* 5 Mr'69 11 : 3-4

Swearing-in of Bihar team put off. *TI* 6 Mr'69 6 : 3-4

Unstable Bihar; editorial. *TI* 31 Jl'69 6 : 1-2

Where do we go from here; editorial. *Janata* 24(24) 6 Jl'69 1-2

Y.B. Chavan deputed to help Bihar leader in forming ministry. *TI* 15 Fe'69 1 : 7-8+

    See also

Communist Party (India)—Bihar unit

Harihar Singh

———— : 1970

Again in the melting pot; editorial. *Janata* 25(23) 28 Je'70 1-2

All-out bid today to throw out Daroga Rai ministry. *TI* 13 Je'70 1 : 5-6

Axis in tight spot. *Link* 12(25) 1 Fe'70 15

Bihar C.M.'s talks with Jagjivan Ram on Govt expansion. *TI* 24 Fe'70 7 : 4-5

Bihar Government in doldrums. *Organiser* 33(40) 16 My'70 2

Bihar Government is voted out of power : CM tenders resignation. *TI* 19 De'70 1 : 1-3

Bihar Governor for extension of President's rule. *TI* 12 Fe'70 1 : 1-3

Bihar ministry survives major trial of strength. *TI* 14 Je'70 1 : 5-6+

Bihar SSP asks for a week's time. *TI* 14 Fe'70 1 : 5-6

Bihar SVD collapses as Ramanand Tiwari gives up leadership. *TI* 8 Fe'70 1 : 1-3

Bihar SVD Govt : How long? *Link* 13(20) 27 De'70 16-17

Bihar SVD repeats its claim. *TI* 15 Fe'70 1 : 5-6+

Bihar : Story of inter-party wrangles. *Janata* 25(6) 1 Mr'70 2-3+

Bihar uncertainty persists. K. Gopalan *New Age* 18(50) 13 De'70 7

Birth of new Government. *Link* 12(28) 22 Fe'70 15-16

Break-up threat to Bihar SVD. *TI* 7 Fe'70   1 : 8+

CPI lashes out at dissident bid to foist-style SVD in Bihar.
New Age 18(46) 15 Nv'70 10

CPI, PSP to support Congress(R) in Bihar. *TI*   13 Fe'70
1 : 2-3+

CPI threat to Bihar Coalition. *TI* 22 Mr'70 5 : 3-4

Caste in Bihar politics. Nagesh Jha *econ and Political Wkly*
5(7) 14 Fe'70 341-44 tabs

Centre had no part in Govt-formation in U.P.; Bihar :
Chavan. *TI* 25 Fe'70 1 : 4-5+

Class, caste-and power. *econ and Political Wkly* 5(25)
20 Je'70 967-69

Congi will lose the Ministry and all the four by-elections in
Bihar. *Organiser* 24(16) 28 Nv'70 2

Congress dissidents still at toppling game. K. Gopalan
New Age 18(47) 22 Nv'70 6

Crisis in most parties. *Link* 12(40) 17 My'70 17-18

Cruel month. *econ and Political Wkly* 5(18) 2 My'70
729-30

Daroga Rai as leader. *Link* 12(23) 18 Ja'70 17

Daroga Rai Govt survives division in Assembly. *TI*
12 Ap'70 1 : 2-3+

Daroga Rai illusions. *Link* 13(9) 11 Oc'70 22-23

Daroga Rai on the mat. *Link* 12(40) 17 My'70 9

End Bihar's impasse; editorial. *New Age* 18(49) 6 De'70 2

Four-party alliance poses challenge to Rai Govt. *TI* 9 Je'70
1 : 1-5

4-party SVD in Bihar takes shape. *TI* 1 Fe'70 9 : 5

A futile exercise; editorial. *TI* 30 Ja'70 6 : 1-2

Ganging-up in Patna; editorial. *New Age* 18(52
27 De'70 2

Government of 'undependables'. *econ and Political Wk'y*
5(10) 7 Mr'70 441-42

Grabbing the flower of power. *Thought* 22(44) 13 Oc'70 7

Harihar Singh and Rai to submit supporters list to the
Governor. *TI* 18 Ja'70 1 : 7-8+

He laughs best who laughs fast. *Organiser* 23(31)
14 Mr'70 3

Hope for stability, none. *Thought* 22(3) 17 Ja'70 10

Ideological rift threatens SVD in Bihar. *TI* 2 Fe'70 1 : 7-8

In a cleft stick; editorial. *TI* 12 Je'70 6 : 1

Is Rai reluctant? *Link* 12(33) 29 Mr'70 14-15

Kaleidoscopic change. L.P. Sinha *Link* 13(1) 15 Ag'70 59-63

Kanungo keen to have stable Govt in Bihar. *TI* 29 Ja'70 5 : 3-4

A make-shift affair; editorial. *TI* 18 Fe'70 8 : 1

Ministry to be expanded later : 3-men Coalition. Govt led by Daroga Rai installed in Bihar. *TI* 17 Fe'70 1 : 1-3

Motley crowd in Bihar ministry—Principles given up; opportunists combine. *New Age* 18(52) 27 De'70 16

Move to topple Daroga Rai—Congress dissidents play reaction's game. *New Age* 18(44) 1 Nv'70 16

Opportunistic Coalitions. *Commerce* 121(3112) 26 De'70 1312-13

PSP and CPI firm in support. *TI* 16 Fe'70 1 : 1+

PSP move to withdraw support to Bihar Govt worries Congress(R). *TI* 21 Mr'70 7 : 1-2

Pandemonium leads to adjournment of Bihar Assembly. *TI* 1 Jl'70 5 : 4-5

Prospects before new ministry. Jagannath Sarkar *Mainstream* 8(39) 30 Mr'70 17-20

Prospects for popular ministry. *Link* 12(21) 4 Ja'70 15-16

Protest against MLA's arrest : SSP walk-out in Bihar Assembly. *TI* 2 Jl'70 5 : 1-2

Rai Govt escapes 'snap' defeat. *TI* 24 Je'70 5 : 1-2

The Rai ministry and PSP. *Janata* 25(6) 1 Mr'70 13

Rai's parleys with Coalition partners. *TI* 24 Oc'70 1 : 5-6

Rethinking follows Rightist bid. *Link* 13(12) 1 Nv'70 13

Rift-riven Coalition in Bihar in difficulty. *TI* 25 My'70 1 : 4-5+

Ruling party hopeful of forming Bihar Govt. *TI* 22 Ja'70 1 : 2-3+

Rumblings of revolt against Bihar C.M. *TI* 27 Mr'70 1 : 5 6+

SSP at breaking point. *Link* 12(27) 15 Fe'70 **12-13**

SSP green signal for Coalition in Bihar. *TI* 6 Fe'70 1 : 2-3+

The S.V.D. in Bihar; editorial. *Political and econ Rev* 1(43) 30 De'70   2

SVD leader invited by Bihar Governor to form ministry. *TI* 22 De'70   1 : 7-8

Shakier than ever. *Link* 13(17)   6 De'70   16-17

Surprising developments favour new Congress. *Commerce* 120(3068)   21 Fe'70   324

Thakur sworn in head of 11-man SVD ministry. *TI* 23 De'70   1 : 7-8+

Tiwari chosen leader of four-party Bihar SVD. *TI* 24 Ja'70 1 : 1-4

To be back is enough. *econ and Political Wkly* 5(14) 4 Ap'70 588-89

Uncertainty in Bihar; editorial. *TI* 21 De'70   6 : 1-2

Vested interest in weak governments. *econ and Political Wkly* 5(46)   14 Nv'70   1839

Where Daroga Rai tripped. **Girish Mishra**   *Mainstream* 9(17)   26 De'70   12+

Will Rai behave?   *Link*   13(13)   8 Nv'70   16-17

    See also

Corruption (in politics)

———— : 1971

Bihar : Alliance and struggle. *Link* 14(8)   3 Oc'71   19

Bihar : CPI warns against Congress-R machinations. *New Age* 19(29)   18 Jl'71   16

Bihar needs a fresh poll; editorial. *TI* 19 My'71   6 : 1

Bihar. *Political and econ Rev* 2(19)   17 Jl'71   9

Bihar SSP faction's threat to quit SVD. *TI* 12 Ap'71 10 : 4-5

Bihar SSP men fight like kilkenny cats. K. Gopalan *New Age* 19(5)   31 Ja'71   5

Bihar SSP Minister quits; socialist group to pull out of Coalition. *TI* 18 My'71   1 : 1-3+

Bihar SVD ministry's fate in balance as 2 more Ministers quit. *TI* 31 My'71   1 : 1-3

Bihar to come under President's rule. *TI* 29 De'71 7 : 5-6

Bihar's crumbling parties : The dynamics of disintegration.
Dilip Mukerjee　*TI*　27 Fe'71　6 : 3-5+

Bihar's plight; editorial.　*TI*　15 Je'71　6 : 1

Bills to lower ceilings and limit urban property. K. Gopalan
New Age　19(27)　4 Jl'71　3

Bitter fruits of opportunism.　*People's Democracy*　7(21)
23 My'71　2

CPI Bloc withdraws support from PVD Ministry in Bihar.
TI　15 Jl'71　1 : 7-8+

CPI outlines conditions to rejoin Bihar PVD.　*New Age*
19(45)　7 Nv'71　1

Coalition in disarray.　*Swarajya*　16(20)　13 Nv'71　14

Congress-CPI discord.　*Link*　13(50)　25 Jl'71　22

Congress(N) signal for PVD ministry in Bihar.　*TI*
26 My'71　1 : 5-6+

Congress(R) claim to form Govt in Bihar upheld by Governor.　*TI*　16 Fe'70　1 : 1-3

The Congress(R) move to unseat the SVD ministry in
Bihar.　*Capital*　166(4156)　25 Mr'71　530

Crisis in Bihar PVD Govt, seems imminent following CPI
threat.　*TI*　12 Jl'71　1 : 5-6

Crisis in Bihar PVD virtually blows over.　*TI*　13 Jl'71
1 : 1-2

An ephemeral stability.　*Thought*　23(51)　18 De'71　9

Four more Bihar Ministers quit on eye of censure move.
TI　1 Je'71　1 : 7-8+

Government's intention to rule by Ordinance.　*Swarajya*
16(8)　21 Ag'71　10

Kapoori goes unsung.　*Link*　13(43)　6 Je'71　19-20

A mystery.　*Link*　13(49)　18 Jl'71　17-18

Nemesis of opportunism.　*People's Democracy*　7(23)　6 Je'71
2+

PSP's future.　*Link*　13(48)　11 Jl'71　20-21

Paswan Govt resigns to pave way for mid-term elections.
TI　28 De'71　1 : 7-8

Paswan may join Congress(N).　*TI*　5 Je'71　1 : 1

Paswan to head PVD ministry in Bihar : Swearing in today.
TI　2 Je'71　1 : 7-8+

Paswan turns down resignation demand. *TI* 16 Jl'71 1 : 1-4+

Reactionary SVD raj in Bihar tumbles. K. Gopalan *New Age* 19(23) 6 Je'71 16

SSP allowed to stay in Bihar SVD Govt. *TI* 2 My'71 1 : 4-5

SVD to PVD; editorial. *TI* 3 Je'71 6 : 1

Tasks for Paswan Govt. *Link* 13(44) 13 Je'71 20

Thakur's future. *Link* 13(39) 9 My'71 16

Threat to Bihar SVD Govt averted : Censure motion is withdrawn. *TI* 2 Ap'71 1 : 7-8+

A time to go; editorial. *TI* 16 Jl'71 6 : 1-2

Timely exit; editorial. *TI* 29 De'71 6 : 1

The toppling game in Bihar. *Commerce* 122(3135) 5 Je'71 1041

Wages of opportunism; editorial. *Mainstream* 9(40) 5 Je'71 5-6

See also

Indian National Congress (New)—Bihar unit

_____ : 1972

Bihar can at last hope to have a stable Govt. *TI* 15 Mr'72 7 : 1-3

Bihar : Opportunism does not pay. *Link* 14(26) 6 Fe'72 25-26

Censure motion against Bihar Govt rejected. *TI* 27 Je'72 1 : 7-8+

Dissolution of Assembly and President's rule. *Swarajya* 16(31) 29 Ja'72 2

Kedar Pande to head Bihar Govt. *TI* 17 Mr'72 1 : 8

Move to send Mishra to Bihar dropped. *TI* 16 Mr'72 1 : 4-5

The opportunist in Bihar Congress. *Link* 14(21) 2 Ja'72 26-27

Political elite in Bihar. Shashishekhar Jha. Vora. 1972, 332p. Rs 25 Review
Eastern Econ 59(9) 1 Se'72 508; *Indian and Foreign Rev* 10(14) 1 My'73 20-21

Politics of coalition governments : The experience of the first United Front Government in Bihar. Haridwar Rai and Jawaharlal Pandey *J Constitutional and Parliamentary Stud* 6(2) Ap-Je'72 48-82 tabs bibliogr-ft-n

Twilight in Bihar; editorial. *TI* 13 Ja'72 4 : 1-2

_____ : 1973

Bihar : Back to square one. *Commerce* 126(3243) 30 Je'73 1280-81

Bihar : Embarrassing defeat. *Link* 16(20) 23 De'73 21-22

The Bihar farce. *Commerce* 126(3239) 2 Je'73 1100-01

Bihar : How Pandey dug his own grave. *Link* 15(47) 1 Jl'73 17-18

Bihar : Rift widens. *Link* 15(33) 25 Mr'73 19-21

Bihar : The gamble that misfired. *Link* 15(43) 3 Je'73 19

Bihar, who is the leader; editorial. *Thought* 25(27) 7 Jl'73 5

Bihar will not suffer the like of Kedar Pande. Jagannath Sarkar *New Age* 21(25) 24 Je'73 16

Both factions for PM selecting new Bihar leaders. *TI* 25 Je'73 1 : 1-3+

Brisk activity in Patna on eve of AICC Official's visit. *TI* 7 Je'73 1 : 7-8+

Curiouser and curiouser; editorial. *TI* 7 Je'73 6 : 1

Despair and hope in Bihar : An end and a beginning. Ajit Bhattacharjea *TI* 17 Se'73 4 : 3-5; 18 Se'73 4 : 3-5

Emerging trends in Bihar politics. J.K.P. Sinha *Indian J Pol Sci* 34(4) Oc-De'73 471-81 tabs

Inglorious exit and after. *Mainstream* 11(44) 30 Je'73 7-8

Kedar Pande given opportunity to prove majority. *TI* 13 Je'73 1 : 7-8+

Kedar Pande not to be replaced : Congress Chief. *TI* 6 Je'73 1 : 1-3

Kedar Pande's mini coup flops : Demands for his exit grows. *New Age* 21(22) 3 Je'73 1

The national scene : Like a fond parent. Sham Lal *TI* 26 Je'73 6 : 3-5

No confidence against Pande ministry. K. Gopalan *New Age* 21(23) 10 Je'73 16

Ominous trends in Bihar Congress. *Link* 16(19) 16 De'73 21-22

Pande agrees to join Ghafoor ministry. *TI* 5 Jl'73 1 : 2-3+

Pande ministry's fate hangs in balance. *Organiser* 26(44) 9 Je'73 4

Mr. Pande quits; editorial. *TI* 26 Je'73 6 : 1

The politics of defection. A.K. Sen *Swarajya* 18(5) 4 Ag'73 14

President's rule for Bihar? S. Kumar Dev *Commerce* 126(3243) 30 Je'73 1282

A temporary expedient; editorial. *TI* 3 Jl'73 6 : 1-2

24 Bihar Ministers resign : Hectic activity by rivals. *TI* 23 Je'73 1 : 7-8+

2 Ministers shun anti-Pande meet. *TI* 21 Je'73 1 : 4-5+

U.P. and Bihar need policy changes, not gimmicks. *New Age* 21(24) 17 Je'73 1+

———— : 1974

Aberrations in Bihar. *Thought* 26(27) 13 Jl'74 9

All power to his elbow. Brahma Prakash Sharma *Janata* 29(28) 15 Ag'74 31-32

All set for a long drawn struggle. *Janata* 29(28) 15 Ag'74 42-43

An awakened people; editorial. *Organiser* 27(35) 6 Ap'74 3

And now Bihar; editorial. *Eastern Econ* 62(12) 22 Mr'74 611

The battle of Patna. Kamala Sinha *Janata* 29(41) 24 Nv'74 16-17

Bihar a crucible; editorial. *Thought* 26(23) 15 Je'74 3-4

Bihar agitation; letter to the editor. *TI* 15 Je'74 6 : 6

Bihar agitation : New phase. Jitendra Singh *TI* 9 Ag'74 4 : 7-8

Bihar and Bombay students. Sonal Parikh and Alpa Kapadia *Janata* 29(28) 15 Ag'74 39-40

Bihar and the democratic machinery. N.G. Goray *Janata* 29(31) 15 Se'74 8-10

Bihar bandh and after. *People's Democracy* 10(41) 13 Oc'74 1+

Bihar 'bandh' passes off peacefully. *TI* 7 Nv'74 1 : 1-2+

Bihar C.M. seeks Bhave's intervention. *TI* 28 Jl'74 1 : 4-5+

Bihar C.M. takes back 5 portfolios. *TI* 9 Oc'74 1 : 1

Bihar Congress Party in disarray. *TI* 16 Oc'74 1 : 2-5+

Bihar : Decisive battle ahead. Indradeep Sinha *New Age* 22(39) 29 Se'74 1+

Bihar gets ready for final rebuff to JP. *New Age* 22(42) 20 Oc'74 1+

Bihar government may have some new faces. *TI* 17 Ap'74 1 : 7-8+

Bihar : Impasse continues. *Commerce* 129(3313) 9 Nv'74 801

Bihar limps back to normalcy : Toll now, 17. *TI* 7 Oc'74 1 : 5-6+

Bihar may be put under Central rule. *TI* 11 Ap'74 1 : 1-3

Bihar movement—A democratic alternative in the making. Somnath Ghosh *Janata* 29(22) 7 Jl'74 4

Bihar movement is reaching out to uproot Indira's corruptocracy.' Kishore Garg *Organiser* 28(14) 16 Nv'74 3+

Bihar movement— Objectives and perspective. S.M. Joshi *Janata* 29(41) 24 Nv'74 5-6+

The Bihar movement : Some questions. Madhu Limaye *Janata* 29(23) 14 Jl'74 4-6

Bihar : Not by police measures alone; editorial. *Commerce* 129(3313) 9 Nv'74 797

Bihar : Purge of corrupt by the corrupt. *Organiser* 27(37) 20 Ap'74 5+

Bihar—Setting a pattern for agitation. S. Harbhajan Singh *Janata* 29(31) 15 Se'74 4-5

Bihar State Committee calls for Left and democratic unity. *People's Democracy* 10(46) 17 Nv'74 6

Bihar students : The capacity to act. *TI* 11 Ag'74 4 : 2-5

Bihar, the beacon; editorial. *Janata* 29(28) 15 Ag'74 3-5

Bihar : The movement continues. *People's Democracy* 10(18) 5 My'74 12

Bihar—The path finder. Naren Das *Janata* 29(39) 10 Nv'74 3-4

Bihar upsurge and the CPM. *Call* 26(4) De'74 4-5

Bihar upsurge; editorial. *Call* 25(8) Ap'74 3-4

A bird's eye view. *Janata* 29(28) 15 Ag'74 35-37

CPB rules out dissolution of Vidhan Sabha. *TI* 7 Je'74 1 : 8+

CPI and Sangh MLAs clash in Bihar. *TI* 26 Mr'74 1 : 7-8+

CPI-Congress joint campaign in Bihar begins. Jagannath Sarkar *New Age* 22(44) 3 Nv'74 16+

CPI dragon bares its fangs in Bihar. *Organiser* 28(14) 16 Nv'74 1-2

CPI views JP's struggle as right reaction conspiracy. *Janata* 29(28) 15 Ag'74 42

CPI will meet JP's threat in Bihar. Yogindra Sharma *New Age* 22(43) 27 Oc'74 4

The challenge of Bihar. Hans Raj Gulati *Janata* 29(35) 13 Oc'74 8-9

Choice in Bihar; editorial. *TI* 12 Je'74 4 : 1-2

Collusion or dialogue; editorial. *Janata* 29(37) 13 Oc'74 1+

Confusion in Bihar. K. Santhanam *Swarajya* 18(50) 15 Je'74 1-2

Cong-I at its wits' end in Bihar. *Organiser* 28(2) 24 Ag'74 1+

Congi farce in Bihar, but how long? *Organiser* 27(42) 1 Je'74 2+

Consequences of the Bihar upsurge. Surendra Mohan *Janata* 29(13) 5 My'74 17-18

Dark fears raging frustrations. *Link* 16(45) 16 Je'74 10-11

Decision on Bihar leadership today. *TI* 23 My'74 1 : 7-8+

Democracy and development : The grassroots experience in India. R.C. Prasad. Rachna. 1971, 336p. Review *Indian J Publ Adm* 20(4) Oc-De'74 901-04

Despite Congress terror, Bihar stir will engulf all India. *Janata* 29(27) 11 Ag'74 5

Dikshit flays opposition for Bihar trouble. *TI* 22 Mr'74 1 : 4-5

Dikshit rules out Bihar Assembly dissolution. *TI* 29 My'74 1 : 4-5

Disillusionment in Bihar. *Link* 16(45) 16 Je'74 8-10

Dissidents summoned to Delhi. *TI* 21 My'74 1 : 3+

Dissolution of Bihar Assembly ruled out. *TI* 4 Se'74
1 : 1-2

Far too many controls : Formidable bias against investment.
Prem Shankar Jha   *TI* 29 Ag'74   4 : 3-5

Feeling of despair; editorial. *TI* 20 Jl'74   4 : 1

The final round of battle in Bihar. George Fernandes
Janata 29(33) 29 Se'74 7+

A flood of doubt and hope. Arvind Narayan Das   *econ
and Political Wkly* 9(37) 14 Se'74 1564-65

Ghafoor faces strong anti-Congress wave. *TI* 22 Fe'74
1 : 2-5+

Ghafoor Govt. in financial mess on the eve of no tax agitation. *Organiser* 27(46) 29 Je'74 5+

Ghafoor Government doomed to collapse. *Organiser* 27(35)
6 Ap'74 2

Govt's fire-power vs. people's will-power. *Organiser* 28(10)
19 Oc'74 1+

Ill-conceived; editorial. *TI* 10 My'74   4 : 1

INTUC and the Bihar movement. *Janata* 29(41) 17 Nv'74
15

In perspective; editorial. *TI* 6 Je'74   4 : 1-2

Inhuman conditions in Bihar camp jail. *TI* 10 Oc'74
1 : 4-5+

Is Bihar heading towards President's rule? *Swarajya* 19(18)
2 Nv'74 22

J.P. denies preaching rebellion. *TI* 21 Oc'74 1 : 2-3+

JP is pointing the way. B. Vivekanandan *Janata* 29(28)
15 Ag'74 13-16

JP on his Bihar movement. *Janata* 29(24) 21 Jl'74 3-4

'JP' threat to gherao Parliament. *TI* 31 Oc'74 1 : 4-6

JP threatens to go on fast. *TI* 18 Je'74 1 : 6-8+

JP unleashes civil war among students. Indradeep Sinha
New Age 22(31) 4 Ag'74 8

JP warns PM against 'playing with fire.' *TI* 8 Oc'74
1 : 2-3+

JP's call to police to-disobey orders. *TI* 29 Jl'74 1 : 7-8+

JP's expanding objectives : Reaction to Congress cynicism.
Ajit Bhattacharjea *TI* 18 Je'74 4 : 3-5

JP's movement : A positive role to play. Brahmanand *Janata* 29(28) 15 Ag'74 27-29

JP's non-violent arson and terror. *New Age* 22(41) 13 Oc'74 1-2

JP's supporters are disenchanted. *TI* 2 Se'74 1 : 5-6+

Jagjiwan poses increasing challenge to Indira. Kishore Garg *Organiser* 28(1) 17 Ag'74 25+

Jayaprakash Narayan on Bihar—A citizen action pamphlet. Despande, Govindrao. 1970, 38p. Rs 2 Review *Commerce* 129(3298) 27 Jl'74 179

Jayaprakash Narayan's new role; editorial. G. Ramachand-ran *Gandhi Marg* 18(3) Jl'74 139-42

Join JP in "do or die" battle for democracy. *Janata* 29(27) 11 Ag'74 4

Largest-ever rally for Assembly dissolution. *Commerce* 128(3292) 15 Je'74 876-77

Light versus darkness. S.M. Joshi *Janata* 29(28) 15 Ag'74 5-8

Marxist call for united Left. *Janata* 29(28) 15 Ag'74 41

Massive procession lathi-charged : JP hurt. *TI* 5 Nv'74 1 : 4-5+

Massive rally against JP agitation. *TI* 17 Nv'74 1 : 5+

Misleading quit. Arvind Narayan Das *econ and Political Wkly* 9(31) 3 Ag'74 1223-24

Mobs manhandle Bihar legislators. *TI* 14 Je'74 1 : 7-8

The mood of the moment. Prem Bhasin *Janata* 29(41) 17 Nv-24 Nv'74 7-9

Mounting tension in Bihar : Rival demonstrations. Jitendra Singh *TI* 1 Je'74 4 : 7-8

Movement of the masses. N.G. Goray *Janata* 29(41) 24 Nv'74 9-12

National calculations. *econ and Political Wkly* 9(23) 8 Je'74 883

The national scene : New season, new flowers. Sham Lal *TI* 4 Jl'74 4 : 3-5

The Neros and heroes of Bihar. Basanta Chandra Ghose *Janata* 29(10) 7 Ap'74 11-12

No 'Gujarat' in Bihar. *Link* 16(39) 5 My'74 23-24

No PCC effort to counter JP-led stir. *TI* 1 Se'74 1 : 2-5+

No way to govern. Romesh Thapar *econ and Political Wkly* 9(17) 27 Ap'74 657-58

On Bihar movement. *People's Democracy* 10(50) 15 De'74 1+

Onward to the next phase; editorial. *Janata* 29(36) 20 Oc'74 1-2

PM against change in Bihar leadership. *TI* 19 Ap'74 1 : 1-2+

Partisan democracy in Bihar; editorial. *Commerce* 129(3314) 16 Nv'74 828

Patna bandh peaceful : Govt offices unaffected. *TI* 6 Nv'74 1 : 1-2+

Patna tense on eve of mass 'dharna.' *TI* 2 Oc'74 1 : 6-7+

People's administration already functioning in three districts. Roxna S. Swamy *Organiser* 28(17) 7 De'74 7+

People's struggle without precedent. Surendra Mohan *Janata* 29(28) 15 Ag'74 21-23

Piquant political situation in Bihar. *Commerce* 128(3284) 20 Ap'74 546

Police, student 'dadas' rule the roast. *TI* 31 Ag'74 1 : 5-6+

The prince saviour of democracy. Brij Mohan Toofan *Janata* 29(28) 15 Ag'74 17-21

Prospects of Bihar movement and JP leadership; editorial. *Call* 26(4) De'74 3-4

Radical alternative and the Bihar struggle. Surendra Mohan *Janata* 29(31) 15 Se'74 5-6

A......rally in Patna; editorial. *Thought* 26(45) 16 Nv'75 3-4

Revolt in slow motion. Arvind Narayan Das *econ and Political Wkly* 9(50) 14 De'74 2049-51

Sarvodaya workers free to join stir. *TI* 13 Jl'74 1 : 7-8+

Satyagraha and Sarvodaya. Vasant Nargolkar *Janata* 29(28) 15 Ag'74 9-10

Second phase; editorial. *TI* 5 Ag'74 4 : 2

Self defeating; editorial. *TI* 22 My'74 4 : 1-2

The significance of Bihar. Prem Bhasin *Janata* 29(28) 15 Ag'74 33-35

The situation in Bihar is to be seen, to be believed. *Organiser* 27(43) 8 Je'74 1-2

Six blind men. Sudhir Sonalkar *econ and Political Wkly* 9(52) 28 De'74 2136-37

Smash it; editorial. *New Age* 22(42) 20 Oc'74 2

Socialists and the Bihar movement. Pannalal Surana *Janata* 29(28) 15 Ag'74 33-35

Stormy opening of Bihar Vidhan Sabha. *TI* 5 De'74 1 : 7-8+

Strangulation of Bihar : Need for a rescue operation. Girilal Jain *TI* 10 Jl'74 4 : 3-5

Strong-arm tactics against the press; editorial. *Thought* 26(36) 14 Se'74 4-5

Task in Bihar; editorial. *TI* 21 Ag'74 4 : 1-2

Telephone exchange blown up at Begusarai. *TI* 3 Oc'74 1 : 5-7+

There's a way out in Bihar; editorial. *Thought* 26(36) 14 Se'74 3-4

To the bitter end; editorial. *TI* 6 Nv'74 4 : 1-2

The tocsin tolls. Sunil Das *Janata* 29(23) 14 Jl'74 11-12

Total bandh in Bihar leads to total confusion in Cong-1 leadership. *Organiser* 28(9) 12 Oc'74 2

Trade unions must join the struggle. *Janata* 29(39) 10 Nv'74 5

Triple alliance; editorial. *Organiser* 28(12) 2 Nv'74 3

Turmoil in Bihar Congress. *Link* 16(44) 9 Je'74 14-15

Turn in Bihar affairs. *Link* 16(44) 9 Je'74 14-15

2 Sarvodaya leaders externed from Bihar. *TI* 27 Oc'74 1 : 1-2+

An uncommon movement; editorial. *econ Affairs* 19(2) De'74 491-93

Undertones of Fascism. *Link* 16(45) 16 Je'74 11-12

Unfortunate; editorial. *TI* 9 My'74 4 : 2

Unrest in Bihar; letter to the editor. *Link* 16(46) 23 Je'74 2-3

Uproarious scenes in Bihar Vidhan Sabha. *TI* 9 Ap'74 1 : 7-8+

The voice of silence. Madhu Dandavate *Janata* 29(28) 15 Ag'74 23-25

A way out; editorial. *TI* 21 Nv'74 4 : 1-2

We cannot sit back. *Janata* 29(28) 15 Ag'74 43

What is really happening in Bihar? Subhash Chandra Sarker *Commerce* 128(3283) 13 Ap'74 494+

What's going on in Bihar. Ajit Bhattacharjea *ill Wkly India* 95(21) 21 Jl'74 4-9

Where democracy is in hidding; editorial. *Thought* 26(45) 16 Nv'74 4-5

Who is to blame in Bihar; editorial. *Eastern Econ* 62(13) 29 Mr'74 643-45

Why students should sacrifice one year of studies. Jayaprakash Narayan *Organiser* 27(50) 27 Jl'74 8-9

Youth revolt in Bihar : Some reflections. Sachchidanand Sinha *Mankind* 18(3) Jl-Se'74 10-16

————— : 1975-

The Bihar and Kerala struggles. E.M.S. Namboodiripad *People's Democracy* 11(2) 12 Ja'75 5+

Bihar Assembly to debate bomb blast. *TI* 14 Fe'75 1 : 1-2+

Bihar C.M. threatens to arrest JP. *TI* 30 Ja'75 1 : 1-2+

Bihar Legislature gets off to noisy start. *TI* 13 Fe'75 1 : 7-8+

Bihar : Mishra starts with big goodwill. P.S. Madan *New Age* 23(20) 18 My'75 11

Bihar : Right steps by new Govt. *Link* 17(40) 18 My'75 15

Bihar sundown. A.K. Sen *Swarajya* 19(48) 31 My'75 9-11

Bihar : The great defreeze. Dev Dutt *Gandhi Marg* 19(1) Ja'75 92-101

CPB decision on Bihar likely on Monday. *TI* 8 Mr'75 1 : 7-8

Challenge in Bihar; editorial. *New Age* 23(13) 30 Mr'75 2

Choice in Bihar; editorial. *TI* 8 Fe'75 6 : 1-2

Decision soon on Bihar leadership : Barooah. *TI* 11 Fe'75 1 : 1-2+

EMS, Jyoti Basu address public rallies. *People's Democracy* 11(1) 5 Ja'75 3

The February lo rally and the tasks ahead. S.S. Shrivastava *People's Democracy* 11(10) 9 Mr'75 9-10

Ghafoor's claim is challenged. *TI* 9 Fe'75 1 : 3+

High Command allows Ghafoor to step down. *TI* 26 Mr'75 1 : 4-5

Ill-advised threat; editorial. *TI* 30 Ja'75 4 : 1

JN Mishra group's threat to boycott Assembly. *TI* 8 Fe'75 1 : 2-3+

JP's government strengthens semifedual bondage. *New Age* 23(17) 27 Ap'75 5

JP's real mission. *econ and Political Wkly* 10(12) 22 Mr'75 509 11 tab

Janata sarkar at Raghopur—A revolution in the making. Amarendra Dhaneshwar *Janata* 30(14) 1975 15-16

Kesari holds talks with party leaders. *TI* 17 Mr'75 1 : 1-2

New alignments in Bihar : Congress infighting. Jitendra Singh *TI* 18 Fe'75 4 : 7-8

No redemption for Bihar yet in sight. *Organiser* 28(27) 15 Fe'75 5

On anti-repression day on the anniversary of the Bihar movement. *People's Democracy* 11(11) 16 Mr'75 1+

Operation 'total revolution'. Janardhan Thakur *econ and Political Wkly* 10(8) 22 Fe'75 344-45

Political elites and modernisation. Ram Ahuja. Meenakshi. Rs 30 Review *TI* 17 Ag'75 6 : 1-3

President's rule in Bihar soon. *Organiser* 28(27) 15 Fe'75 1-2

Pro-changers in Bihar bow to Central leadership. *TI* 10 Fe'75 1 : 1-2

Pro-changers relent at Dikshit's intervention. *TI* 12 Fe'75 1 : 2-3+

Status quo continues. *Commerce* 130(3334) 12 Ap'75 512-13

Uncertainty in Bihar. *Link* 17(25) 2 Fe'75 22

POPULATION

*Bihar population problems. S.R. Bose. A.N. Sinha Inst of Soc Stud. 1969, 87p. Rs 15

Findings of 1971 census in Bihar. B.L. Das *Commerce (Suppl)* 127(3263) 17 Nv'73 45-49 tabs

Growth of population in the lower Ganga-Ghaghar Doab. Ram Niwas Misra *Indian Geographical J* 45(1-2) Ja-Mr-Ap-Je'70 27-32 bibliogr

Population growth at two Santhal villages at Bihar. Jayanta Sarkar *Vanyajati* 18(4) Oc'70 166-69 tabs bibliogr-ft-n

Some aspects of fertility in a social group of India. M.L. Srivastava *J soc Res* 12(2) Se'69 61-70 bibliogr tabs

21.38% rise in Bihar's population. *TI* 19 Ap'71 10 : 3

See also

Family planning

POTTERY

Ancient handicrafts. P.L. Gupta *Marg* 20(1) De'66 13-15

PRAJA Socialist Party : Bihar unit

Coalition at the Centre soon-Dwivedy. *Janata* 23(45) 8 De'68 15

Facts behind Babu's defection. *Janata* 25(25) 12 Jl'70 4

PSP decides to join ministry in Bihar. *Janata* 23(16) 12 My'68 13-14

PSP list for mid-term poll in Bihar. *TI* 2 Ja'69 3 : 6

PSP's double-dealing. *Link* 11(18) 15 De'68 10

PRASAD, Awadhesh

    See Rai, Haridwar jt. auth.

PRASAD, C.

    See Singh, N.P. jt. auth.

PRASAD, Harish Chandra

A bibliography of folkloristic studies in Bihar : Books, articles, reports and monographs in English and Hindi. *Folklore* 11(7) Jl'70 258-71; 11(9) Se'70 334-40; 11(10) Oc'70 369-83

PRASAD, Kedarnath

Bihar's trade economic growth : Diagnosis and prescription. *Southern Econ* 12(21) 1 Mr'74 19-22

The economics of a backward region in a backward economy : A case study of Bihar in relation to other states of India. Scientific bk Ag. xvi, 584p. Rs 45 Review *AICC econ Rev* 20(19) 15 Ap'69 33; *Commerce* 118(3030) 31 My'69 1088; *Eastern Econ* 52(4) 24 Ja'69 142-43; *Indian J Econ* 48(4) Ap'68 498; *Link* 11(31) 16 Mr'69 48; *Mainstream* 6(50) 10 Ag'68 36-38

PRASAD, L.B.

"Three tier panchayat system of Santhals." *Vanyajati* 20(1) Ja'72 46-49

PRASAD, M.M.

Bihar State Co-operative Land Mortgage Bank and supply of credit. *Indian J Commerce* 21(2) Je'68 31-39

PRASAD, P.K.

See Singh, M.L. jt. auth.

PRASAD, Pradhan H.

Agrarian unrest and economic change in rural Bihar : Three case studies. *econ and Political Wkly* 10(24) 14 Je'75 931-37 tabs ft-n

Production relations : Achilles' heel of Indian planning. *econ and Political Wkly* 8(19) 12 My'73 869-72 bibliogr-ft-n

The semi-proletariat of rural Bihar. *Call* 26(4) De'74 8-13 tabs

Towards an approach to the fifth plan for Bihar. *Mankind* 16(1) Ag-Oc'72 27-33

PRASAD, R.C.

Democracy and development : The grassroots experience in India. Rachna. 1971, 336p. Review
Indian J Publ Adm 20(4) Oc-De'74 901-04

PRASAD, S.M.

Some growth points for the development of chemical and allied industries in Bihar. *Bihar Inform* 18(2) 26 Ja'70 31-32

PRESS

Bihar press in nation's freedom movement. Chandradip Sahay *Bihar Inform* 18(17) 1 Oc'70 6+

What ails the Bihar press. Subhash Chandra Sarkar *Vidura* 7(2) My'70 17-20

PRICES

Index fraud in Bihar exposed : AITUC demands tripartite investigation committee. K. Gopalan *New Age* 13(10) 7 Mr'75 5

Masses act against price rise. K. Gopalan *New Age* 14(15) 10 Ap'66 7

PUBLIC administration

Administration of a state as seen by a Governor. M. Ananthasayanam Ayyangar *Eastern Econ* 52(16) 18 Ap'69 814-18

PUBLIC sector enterprises

State undertakings in Bihar and their profitability. Raj Kishore Sinha *Bihar Inform* 18(8) 1 My'70 1-4

PUBLIC service commissions

Government vs. P.S.C.   *Link*   8(44)   12 Je'66   16-17

QEYAMUDDIN AHMAD

A view of the provincial administration of Bihar under Farrukhsiyar, 1712-19.   *J Bihar Res Soc*   50(1-4)   Ja-De'64   114-24

RAI, Binay Kumar

Man and forest in Chotanagpur.   *Vanyajati*   16(3)   Jl'68   85-92

RAI, Haridwar

Co-ordination of development programme at the district level with special reference to the role of the district officers in Bihar.   *Indian J Publ Adm*   12(1)   Ja-Mr'66   28-59   bibliogr-ft-n

———— and Awadhesh Prasad

Reorganising panchayats raj in Bihar.   A critique of the reform proposals.   *Indian J Publ Adm*   21(1)   Ja-Mr'75   19-47   ft-n

———— and Pandey, Jawaharlal

Politics of coalition governments : The experience of the first United Front Government in Bihar.   *J Constitutional and Parliamentary Stud*   6(2)   Ap-Je'72   48-82   tabs   bibliogr-ft-n

RAJGIR

Rajgir and its surroundings.   R. Bhattacharyya and U. Sen   *Geographical Rev India*   28(2)   Je'66   41-46

RAM KUMAR

See   Mahmood, A. jt. auth.

RAMACHANDRAN, G.

Jayaprakash Narayan's new role; editorial.   *Gandhi Marg*   18(3)   Jl'74   139-42

RAMACHANDRAN, K.S.

Assessing the prospects for Heavy Engineering Corporation.   *Capital*   162(4043)   2 Ja'69   19-20

RAMAN, Revati

*Bihar sales tax manual, containing Bihar Sales Tax Act, 1959 with rules, forms, notifications, comments and case laws.   Pahuja Brothers.   1963,   vi, 292p.   Rs 14

RAMESHWAR SINGH

Maize seed production in Bihar.   *Bihar Inform*   18(11)   16 Je'70   5-8   tabs   appdx

RANCHI : Communal riots

Behind communal riots in Ranchi, Jana Sangh, Congress anti-Urdu collusion. *New Age* 15(36) 3 Se'67 7

The bitter truth about Ranchi. *Organiser* 21(5) 10 Se'67 1-2

How Ranchi blew up...... *Organiser* 21(7) 24 Se'67 16

Ranadive shows no respect for truth in villifying CPI, Unni Krishnan *New Age* 15(40) 1 Oc'67 7+

The Ranchi Report. *Organiser* 22(11) 26 Oc'68 3

Ranchi rioting. *Link* 10(4) 3 Se'67 15

Ranchi riots : Factural analysis of the tragic happenings in Ag'67. Sampradayikta Vir Comm. Review *Seminar* 106 Je'68 48-49

Ranchi's danger signal; editorial. *New Age* 15(36) 3 Se'67 2

Sinister forces behind holocaust. *New Age* 15(37) 10 Se'67 13

_____ : History

The changing face of Ranchi. L.P. Vidyarthi *ill Wkly India* 89(11) 17 Mr'68 43 ills

RANCHI University

Geography of Ranchi university. E Ahmad *Geographical Rev India* 33(1) Mr'68 33-40 tabs bibliogr

RANJAN, C N.

Six guilty men of Bihar; Aiyar Commission findings. *Organiser* 23(28) 21 Fe'70 4+

RAO, K.L.

Flood situation in Bihar. *Bihar Inform* 17(15) 1 Se'69 15

RAO, T.S. and Bogaert, M.V.D.

The beggar problem in Ranchi. *Indian J soc Wk* 31(3) Oc'70 285-302 tabs bibliogr-ft-n appdx

RAVINDRA KISHORE

How the Mishra family looted Kosi Project. *Organiser* 27(5) 8 Se'73 5

RAY, Alaknanda and Ray, Gautamsankar

A technical study of some prehistoric potsherds. *Man in India* 43(2) Ap-Je'63 147-54 bibliogr

RAY, Gautamsankar

See Ray, Alaknanda. jt. auth.

RAZI AHMED

The stain of Indigo and birth of satyagraha in India. *Bihar Inform* 18(14) 15 Ag'70 24-28

REGIONAL planning

Regional planning in Bihar. M.P. Pandey *Eastern Econ* 63(6) 9 Ag'74 243-47 tabs

RELE, Subhash J.

Heavy Engineering Corporation in a mess. *Swarajya* 17(5) 29 Jl'72 9-10

REVENUE

Resource mobilisation in Bihar : 1951-73. Bireshwar Ganguly *Commerce (Suppl)* 127(3263) 17 Nv'73 79-83 tabs bibliogr

RICE

Bihar rice for China; editorial. *Organiser* 18(44) 14 Je'65 3

Scope for expansion of high-yielding varieties in Bihar. S.C. Mandal and V.R. Kulkarni *Indian Fmg* 21(7) Oc'71 104-05

Study of marketable surplus of paddy in Shahabad district. P.N. Bhargava and others *econ Affairs* 20(1-2) Ja-Fe'75 56-64 tabs bibliogr

RIOTS

And now Bihar; editorial. *Eastern Econ* 62(12) 22 Mr'74 611

Army out in Patna after mob violence, property worth crores destroped : Five killed in police firing. *TI* 19 Mr'74 1 : 2-3+

Arson, looting unabated in Bihar towns. *TI* 21 Mr'74 1 : 1-2+

Bihar takes the people's struggle forward. S.S. Srivastava *People's Democracy* 10(14) 7 Ap'74 12

Bihar's ordeal; editorial. *TI* 20 Mr'74 4 : 1

Politicians on student's bandwagon. *Commerce* 128(3280) 23 Mr'74 368-69

3 killed in Gaya firing on students. *TI* 13 Ap'74 1 : 7-8

Violence politically motivated : Dikshit. *TI* 21 Mr'74 1 : 2-3

Violence spreads in Bihar : 10 killed in firing. *TI* 20 Mr'74 1 : 1-3+

RITES and ceremonies

Rites and rituals : Media of rural integration. Kumarananda Chattopadhyay *Eastern Anthropologist* 23(3) Se-De'70 217-33 tabs bibliogr

RIVER-VALLEY projects

For power and irrigation. *Link* 7(23) 17 Ja'65 27

River basin development aid to economic prosperity. K L. Rao *Assam Inform* 19(6) Se'68 33-34

River-valley projects. T.P. Singh *ill Wkly India* 89(12) 24 Mr'69 22-23

RIVERS

*Janakapur paricaya. Jivanath Jha. Darbhanga press co. ii, 34p. ills 21.5cm. Rs 1.25

ROADS

Higher priority needed for development of roads in coalfield areas. *Capital* 165(4129) 3 Se'70 415

RODGERS, G B.

Effects of public works on rural poverty : Some case studies from the Kosi area of Bihar. *econ and Political Wkly (Annual Number)* 8(4-6) Fe'73 255-68 tabs bibliogr-ft-n

ROTHERMUND, Indira

Women in a coal-mining district. *econ and Political Wkly* 10(31) 2 Ag'75 1160-65 tabs bibliogr-ft-n

ROY, Daroga Prasad

Code of discipline and industrial peace in Bihar. *Indian Lab J* 4(3) Mr'63 237-39

ROY, Kalyan

Coal miners resist owners' repression. *New Age* 15(19) 7 My'67 6

ROY, N.K. and others

An analysis of economic structure of East Bihar villages. *Khadi Gramodyog* 21(7) Ap'75 349-53 tabs

ROY, Prakash

United strike against wage-cut in BSP mine. *New Age* 15(25) 18 Je'67 7

ROY, Ramashray
Bihar. *Seminar* 95 Jl'67 35-41 tabs

Conflict and cooperation in a North Bihar village. *J Bihar Res Soc* 49 Ja-De'63 297-315

ROY, Ratan

Pay Committee's fantastic wisdom : Bihar Govt. employees plan to fight back retrograde Report. *New Age* 12(44) 1 Nv'64 15

ROY, Sarat Chandra

The Mundas and their country. Asia. 1970, 407p. Rs 40 Review
Indian Librarian 25(4) Mr'71 225

ROY CHOUDHURY, P.C.

Cottage industries of tribal Chota Nagpur. *Khadi Gramodyog* 13(6) Mr'67 462-64

The creation of Santhal Parganas. *Bengal Past & Present* 81(1) Ja-Je'62 50-56

*Folk tales of Bihar. Sahitya Akad. 1970, xxiv, 132p. Rs 8

Impact of community development on tribal community. *Khadi Gramodyog* 13(9) Je'67 657-60

RURAL conditions

Agrarian unrest and economic change in rural Bihar : Three case studies. Pradhan H. Prasad *econ and Political Wkly* 10(24) 14 Je'75 931-37 tabs ft-n

An analysis of economic structure of East Bihar villages. N.K. Roy and others *Khadi Gramodyog* 21(7) Ap'75 349-53 tabs

Conflict and cooperation in a North Bihar village. Ramashray Roy *J Bihar Res Soc* 49 Ja-De'63 297-315

Effects of public works on rural poverty : Some case studies from the Kosi area of Bihar. G.B. Rodgers *econ and Political Wkly (Annual Number)* 8(4-6) Fe'73 255-68 tabs bibliogr-ft-n

Impact of Kosi embankment : A study of two villages in North Bihar. N.K. Jaiswal and U.K. Vyas *econ and Political Wkly* 4(47) 22 Nv'69 1821-22 tabs

Levels of living in rural areas in Bihar. C.P. Shastri *Indian J agric Econ* 18(1) Ja-Mr'63 302-10 tabs

Levels of living in rural areas : U. Sen Karanayanan. *Indian J agric Econ* 18(1) Ja-Mr'63 341-48 tabs

Levels of living in rural household. Satish Chandra Jha *Indian J agric Econ* 18(1) Ja-Mr'63 311-16 tabs

The Musahri plan : A step towards district planning; editorial. *Voluntary Action* 13(4) Jl-Ag'71 1-2

The semi-proletariat of rural Bihar. Pradhan Prasad *Call*
26(4) De'74 8-13 tabs

A vital experiment; editorial. *Voluntary Action*   13(4)
Jl-Ag'71 2 Repr

> *See also*

Unemployment, Rural

RURAL electrification

Economics of rural electrification in Bihar.   B.N. Sahu
Indian J agric Econ 24(4) Oc-De'69 191

Rural electrifications and employment with special reference to Bihar. Rajkishore Sinha *Bihar Inform* 18(5)
16 My'70 9-11

RURAL industries

Buxar Project. *Kurukshetra* 18(4) Ja'70 29-30+

Development of khadi and village industries in Bihar.
Siddheswar Prasad *Khadi Gramodyog* 21(1) Oc'74 21-22

Dumka Project in Bihar. *Kurukshetra* 17(10) Jl'69 18-20

Ranchi Project. J.L. Saaz *Yojana* 11(12) 25 Je'67 29-30;
11(13) 9 Jl'67 29-32

Rural industries project, Nawadah 1962-71. *Voluntary
Action* 14(4-5) Jl-Oc'72 20-31 tabs

Secret of Nawadah's success. *Kurukshetra* 16(10) Jl'68
19-24 ills

SACHCHIDANANDA

Caste and conflict in Bihar village. *Eastern Anthropologist*
20(2) My-Ag'67 143-50 bibliogr

*Culture change in tribal Bihar, Munda and Oraon. Book-
land. 1964, ii, 158p. Rs 12

Emergent scheduled caste elite in Bihar. *Religion and Soc*
21(3) Se'74 55-61

Impact of industrialization on Bihar tribes. *Cultural Forum*
7(1-2) Ap'65 20-24

Impact of the struggle for freedom on the socio-economic
structure in Bihar. *Bihar Inform* 18(4) 15 Ag'70 56-59

The internal colony. Sindhu Pub. 1973, vi, 159p. Rs 25
Review
Sociological Bull 23(1) Mr'74 144-47

A novel experiment in Bihar. *Commerce (Suppl)* 127(3263)
17 Nv'73 69-73

Social dimensions of agricultural development. National Pub H. 1972, 195p. Rs 30 Review
Behavioural Sci and Community Development 7(1) Mr'73 74-77; *soc Action* 23(1) Ja-Mr'73 110-11

The struggle for freedom. *ill Wkly India* 89(11) 17 Mr'68 15-17 ills

Tribal culture. *Marg* 20(1) De'66 55-60 ills

*Tribal village in Bihar. Munshiram. 281p. Rs 24

Youth revolt in Bihar : Some reflections. *Mankind* 18(3) Jl-Se'74 10-16

_____ and Iyer Gopal, K.

Caste tension in Patna. *Eastern Anthropologist* 22(3) Se-De'69 327-48 tabs bibliogr

SADIQ ALI

The drought in Bihar and U.P.; editorial. *AICC econ Rev* 18(10) 1 De'66 3-4

SAHA, Nirmal Kanti

Some aspects of the Santhals supernatural world and the go-between. *Vanyajati* 18(4) Oc'70 182-86

SAHAI, S.N.

The Khuda Bakhsh Oriental Public Library. *ill Wkly India* 88(38) 22 Oc'67 26-27 ills

SAHAY, B.N.

Pahariyas and their customs. *Vanyajati* 14(1) Ja'66 7-18 ft-n

_____ and Singh, B.K.

Political consciousness among the tribals and their representation in Gram Panchayats *Vanyajati* 18(1) Ja'70 12-16 tabs

SAHAY, Chandradip

Bihar press in nation's freedom movement. *Bihar Inform* 18(17) 1 Oc'70 6+

SAHAY, K.B.

Bihar Congress bid to reduce elections to farce. K. Gopalan *New Age* 15(7) 12 Fe'67 6

End gangster regime; editorial. *New Age* 15(3) 15 Ja'67 2

How corrupt is K.B.? 400 page memo against Bihar Chief Minister submitted to President. *Organiser* 18(21) 4 Ja'65 1-2

Land legislation must be strictly enforced in Bihar. *Political and econ Rev* 1(27) 7 Se'70 7

Pre-primary education, inaugural speech at the national symposium. *Indian Educ* 5(1-2) De'65-Ja'66 28-31

Sahay's bid to prevent free poll. K.U. Warier *New Age* 15(7) 12 Fe'67 3

Sahay's farewell gift to Birlas unearthed. *New Age* 15(20) 14 My'67 1

SAHAY, Keshari N.

Caste and occupation in a village in Bihar. *Man in India* 47(3) Jl-Se'67 178-88 bibliogr-ft-n

Some aspects of interactional pattern at village Kanchampura. *Indian Sociological Bull* 5(1) Oc'67 1-10

SAHI, S.P.

Forest conservation and lac in Bihar. *Foreign Trade of India* 13 My'64 48

SAHU, B.N

Economics of rural electrification in Bihar. *Indian J agric Econ* 24(4) Oc-De'69 191

Peep into productivity in Bihar. *Productivity* 6(2-3) 1965 368-69

Perspective of power development in Bihar. *AICC econ Rev* 18(17) 15 Mr'67 37-39

SAILESHWAR PRASAD

Kurwa : The shifting cultivation of the Maler. *Vanyajati* 19(2-3) Ap Jl'71 95-100 bibliogr

SAKSENA, D.N.

Vasectomy : Field experience of a district hospital in Bihar. *J Family Welfare* 18(2) De'71 9-19 tabs ft-n

SALES tax

Sales tax in Bihar. Ramchandra Prasad Singh *Bihar Inform* 18(20) 1 De'74 9-11

_____ : Law

*Bihar sales tax manual, containing Bihar Sales Tax Act, 1959 with rules, forms, notifications, comments and case laws. Revati Raman. Pahuja Brothers. 1963, vi, 292p. Rs 14

SAMYUKTA Socialist Party : Bihar unit

Bihar SSP at crossroads; too many factions. Jitendra Singh *TI* 17 My'69 6 : 7-8

Bihar SSP to continue basic policy of non-Congressism. *TI* 6 My'69 5 : 2-3

SSP renews claim to from Govt in Bihar. *TI* 3 De'69
1 : 8+

SANTALS, The

Comparative analysis of death rates among the Santals of
two Bihar villages. Jayanta Sarkar   *Man in India* 51(2)
Ap-Je'71 142-50 tabs bibliogr

The creation of Santhal Parganas. P.C. Roy Choudhury
Bengal Past & Present 81(1) Ja-Je'62 50-56

Cruel exploitation; editorial. *TI* 5 De'71 8 : 1

Population growth at two Santhal villages at Bihar. Jayanta
Sarkar *Vanyajati* 18(4) Oc'70 166-69 tabs bibliogr-ft-n

Some aspects of the Santhals supernatural world and the
go-between. Nirmal Kanti Saha *Vanyajati* 18(4) Oc'70
182-86

SANTHANAM, K.

Confusion in Bihar. *Swarajya* 18(50) 15 Je'74 1-2

SANYAL, Suprakash

Ramchand Pandit's Report on opium cultivation in 18th
century Bihar. *Bengal Past & Present* 87(2)   Jl-De'68
181-89 bibliogr-ft-n

SARAN, A.B.

Murder among the Munda : A case study. *Indian J soc Wk*
23(1) Ap'62 1-7

SARKAR, J.N. and Jha, J.C.

A history of the Patna College (1863-1963). Patna College.
1963, i-iv, 170p. Review
J Asiatic Soc (Bengal) 7(1-2) 1965 107

SARKAR, Jagannath

Abolition of Tata zamindari. *Mainstream* 8(44) 4 Jl'70
19-22

Agricultural workers' struggle. *New Age* 12(31) 2 Ag'64 2

Bihar continuing battle. *New Age* 21(14) 8 Ap'73 6

Bihar will not suffer the like of Kedar Pande. *New Age*
21(25) 24 Je'73 16

CPI-Congress joint campaign in Bihar begins. *New Age*
22(44) 3 Nv'74 16+

Coalition government must survive. *New Age* 15(34)
20 Ag'67 3

Poised for another crushing blow to Congress. *New Age*
17(5) 2 Fe'69 3

Problems and prospects of Bihar SVD Government. *New Age* 16(23) 9 Je'68 9+

Prospects before new ministry. *Mainstream* 8(39) 30 My'70 17-20

Tata zamindari must go. *New Age* 19(46) 14 Nv'71 6; 19(47) 21 Nv'71 6

SARKAR, Jayanta

Comparative analysis of death rates among the Santals of two Bihar villages. *Man in India* 51(2) Ap Je'71 142-50 tabs bibliogr

Population growth at two Santhal village at Bihar. *Vanyajati* 18(4) Oc'70 166-69 tabs bibliogr-ft-n

A Santhal view of birth restraints : A case study. *J Family Welfare* 17(1) Se'70 44-47 tabs

SARKAR, R.M.

S C. Roy's approach to the study of the tribal people in Chotanagpur. *Vanyajati* 20(3-4) Jl-Oc'72 122-27

SARKER, S.C.

Violence in Bihar on polling day. *ill Wkly India* 90(9) 2 Mr'69 14

SARKER, Subhash Chandra

Bihar's state income and industrialization. *mod Rev* 127(3) Se'70 179-84 tabs bibliogr-ft-n

Economic condition of North Bihar. *mod Rev* 124(2) Fe'69 121-28; 124(3) Mr'69 183-89 tabs

Industrial profile of states-3—Bihar : Politics hinders development. *Commerce (Annual Number)* 117(3009) 1968 240-45 tab

Tana Bhagat movement. *mod Rev* 130(1) Ja'72 22-26

What ails the Bihar press. *Vidura* 7(2) My'70 17-20

What is really happening in Bihar? *Commerce* 128(3283) 13 Ap'74 494+

SARMA, I. Karthikeya

Bihar stone pillar inscriptions—A revised study. *J orient Inst* 17(3) Mr'68 267-74 bibliogr

SCHEDULED castes and scheduled tribes

Backward classes body to be set up. *TI* 17 Mr'71 7 : 1

Bid to burn alive 26 Harijan families : 10 held. *TI* 3 Je'75 1 : 6-7

Emergent scheduled caste elite in Bihar. Sachchidananda
Religion and Soc   21(3)   Se'74   55-61

How Harijans suffer : Prejudice and persecution. Inder
Malhotra   *TI*   19 Jl'73   6 : 3-5

Our brothers and slaves; editorial.   *Janata*   28(16)
20 My'73   1

Social distance between scheduled castes and upper castes
in East Bihar villages. P.P. Jha and N.K. Jaiswal   *Bihar
Inform*   17(21)   16 De'69   4-6

SEED industry and trade

Experiences in seed production in Bihar.   D.R. Mishra
Bihar Inform   18(7)   16 Ap'70   3-4

SEN, A.K.

Ban on sale of farm land in Bihar. *Swarajya*   15(43)
24 Ap'71   12

Bihar sundown. *Swarajya*   19(48)   31 My'75   9-11

Bihar's murky politics. *Swarajya*   12(13)   23 Se'67   9-10

The foodgrains fiasco. *Swarajya*   17(46)   12 My'73   19

Political outlook in Bihar.   *Swarajya*   12(4)   20 Ap'68
21-22

The politics of defection. *Swarajya*   18(5)   4 Ag'73   14

Requiem for an era. *Swarajya*   12(35)   24 Fe'68   3-4

SEN, Jyoti

Community development in Chotanagpur. Asiatic Soc.
1968, vii, 100p. Rs 16 Review
Man in India   51(1)   Ja-Mr'71   80

SEN, S.N.

Investment on farm and capital formation in agriculture in
Bihar. *Indian J agric Econ*   20(1)   Ja-Mr'65   163-66   tab

Nature and role of the risk and uncertainty in agricultural
production in Bihar. *Indian J agric Econ*   19(1)   Ja-Mr'64
107-09

SEN, U.

     See Bagchi, K. jt. auth.

SENGUPTA, A.K.

Economic organisation of an Oraon village. *Vanyajati*
13(2)   Ap'65   41-45

SENGUPTA, Gita

Addenda to a bibliography of folklore studies in Bihar.
Folklore   11(12)   De'70   452-71

SENGUPTA, J.M. and others

Experimental land utilisation surveys in cadastrally un-surveyed areas through direct plot to plot observations, Bihar 1956-57. *Sankhya (B)* 26(1-2) Nv'64 69-88 tabs

SERICULTURE

Sericulture programmes in Bihar. *Bihar Inform* 17(21) 16 De'69 23-24

SHAHI, S.P.

Bihar bid to preserve wild life. *TI (Suppl)* 24 Nv'69 17 : 3-6

The state's forest wealth. *ill Wkly India* 89(11) 17 Mr'68 45-46

SHAM LAL

The national scene : Like a fond parent. *TI* 26 Je'73 6 : 3-5

The national scene : New season, new flowers. *TI* 4 Jl'74 4 : 3-5

SHARMA, A.P.

Anatomy of a University in Bihar. *Mainstream* 7(27) 8 Mr'69 35-36

SHARMA, B.B.L.

See Jain, P.K. jt. auth.

SHARMA, B.D.

Hurdles to flow of farm credit through co-operatives in Bihar. *Southern Econ* 10(15) 1 De'71 27-28

Some aspects of agricultural credit cooperatives in Bihar. *Indian Cooperative Rev* 7(3) Ap'70 428-32

SHARMA, Beni Shankar

Large-scale voting in Bihar. *Organiser* 22(31) 15 Mr'69 11 +

SHARMA, Brahma Prakash

All power to his elbow. *Janata* 29(28) 15 Ag'74 31-32

SHARMA, D.P.

On developing pharmaceutical industry. *Commerce (Suppl)* 127(3263) 17 Nv'73 25-27

SHARMA, Dasharatha

The account of the Ujjainiyas before their migration to Bihar. *J Bihar Res Soc* 49 Ja-De'63 197-99

SHARMA, H.P.

Rains not enough, but crop prospects not bad. *Yojana* 10(15) 7 Ag'66 5-6

SHARMA, M.L.

   See Singh, C.D. jt. auth.

SHARMA, M.R.N.

   Pilot literacy project in Bihar. *Indian J Adult Educ* 28(3) Mr'67 16

SHARMA, P. Dash

   See Vidyarthi, L.P. jt. auth.

SHARMA, Yogindra

   CPI will meet JP's threat in Bihar. *New Age* 22(43) 27 Oc'74 4

   Joint front against Sahay clique : New development in Bihar political scene. *New Age* 13(51) 19 De'65 14

SHASTRI, C.P.

   Investment on farm and capital formation in agriculture with particular reference to Bihar. *Indian J agric Econ* 20(1) Ja-Mr'65 174-83 tabs

   Levels of living in rural areas in Bihar. *Indian J agric Econ* 18(1) Ja Mr'63 302-10 tabs

SHAW, P.S.

   Need for water pollution control. *Commerce* 118(3027) 16 Se'69 9-11

SHRIVASTAVA, S.S.

   The February 10 rally and the tasks ahead. *People's Democracy* 11(10) 9 Mr'75 9-10

SHUKLA, B.N.

   A study of trade unions in Bihar. *Indian J Lab Econ* 11(3-4) Oc'68-Ja'69 C165-C76 tabs bibliogr-ft-n

SHUKLA, Prabha

   See Verma, K.K. jt. auth.

SIDDHESHWAR PRASAD

   Development of Khadi and village industries in Bihar. *Khadi Gramodyog* 21(1) Oc'74 21-22

SILK manufacture and trade

   Silk industry in Bhagalpur. R.P. Sinha and Anil Kumar *Deccan Geographer* 9(2) Jl-De'71 205-16 tabs maps bibliogr

   Silk industry in Bihar. Jai Narain Thakar *J Bihar Res Soc* 58(1-4) Ja-De'72 285-313 tabs bibliogr-ft-n

SIMHA, Revatiramanprasad

   *Sarapanca ka adhikar aur kartavya. Pahuja Brothers. (H). 1951, ii, 56p. 22cm. Rs 1.25

SIMHA, Vindhyesvariprasad
*Bharatiya kala ko Bihar ki den. Bihar Rashtrabhasha Parishad. (H). 1958, xx, 203p. pls

SINGH, A.K.
Problems and possibilities of growing sugarbeet in Bihar. *Farmer and Parliament* 9(3) Mr'74 7-8+ tabs

_____ and Singh, R.P.
Comparative analysis of role expectations and role performances of subject matter specialists in package and non-package districts. *Indian J Adult Educ* 34(6) Je'73 11-13 tabs

SINGH, B.K.
            See Sahay, B N. jt. auth.

SINGH, B.P.
            See Singh, R.N.P. jt. auth.

SINGH, C.D. and Sharma, M.L.
Institutional financing of industrial development in Bihar. *Southern Econ* 13(15) 1 De'74 11-13 tabs

SINGH, Chandra Shekhar
Strategy of industrial growth. *Commerce (Suppl)* 127(3263) 17 Nv'73 7-11

SINGH, D.P.
*Towns of Uttar Pradesh, Bihar and Madhya Pradesh. Inst of Public Adm (Lucknow Univ). 139p. Rs 10

SINGH, Deoki Nandan
In drought-stricken Bihar. *ill Wkly India* 87(52) 25 De'66 24-25

Introducing India-12 : Bihar. *ill Wkly India* 88(40) 5 Nv'67 28-31 ills

SINGH, Jitendra
Bihar SSP at crossroads; too many factions. *TI* 17 My'69 6 : 7-8

Grain markets for Bihar held up land acquisition hurdle. *TI* 15 Jl'75 4 : 7-8

Patna citizen's ordeal by water. *TI* 30 Ag'75 7 : 1-4

SINGH, K.K.
            See Singh, M.L. jt. auth.

SINGH, M.L.
Unemployment in rural areas of Palamau district (Bihar) : A case study in Hussainabad block. *Indian J agric Econ* 27(4) Oc-De'72 190-98 tabs

_____ and Prasad, P.K.

Evaluation of irrigation schemes in Palamau district (Bihar) : A case study. *Indian J agric Econ* 28(4) Oc-De'73 235-36

_____ and Singh, K.K.

Factors determining agricultural wages : A case study. *Indian J agric Econ* 29(3) Jl-Se'74 54-60 tabs bibliogr-ft-n

SINGH, Madan Mohan

A note on the topography of ancient Rajariha. *J Bihar Res Soc* 50(1-4) Ja-De'64 23-26 bibliogr-ft-n

SINGH, N.K.

Cesspools of unlearning in Bihar. *Swarajya* 16(52) 24 Je'72 2-3

Many faces of caste politics. *econ and Political Wkly* 7(15) 8 Ap'72 748-49

Medical colleges or teaching shops? *econ and Political Wkly* 7(19) 6 Mr'72 920

River of scandal. *econ and Political Wkly* 8(37) 15 Se'73 1673-74

The seven blind men. *econ and Political Wkly* 8(18) 5 Mr'73 824-25

Syndrome of underdevelopment. *econ and Political Wkly* 7(38) 10 Se'72 1909-10

SINGH, N.P. and others

Value orientations of farmers regarding rural living and farming. *Khadi Gramodyog* 18(9) Je'72 519-27 tabs

_____ and Prasad, C.

Selective perception and adoption behaviour of adult farmers. *Indian J Adult Educ* 35(1) Ja'74 14-16 tabs

SINGH, P.B.

Distribution of castes and search for a new theory of caste ranking : Case of the Saran plain. *nat Geographical J India* 21(1) Mr'75 20-46 tabs figs bibliogr-ft-n

SINGH, R.C.

Outsiders in the labour unions in Bihar (a survey of outside leaders in the labour unions in the state of Bihar). *Indian J Lab Econ* 9(4) Ja'67 532-44 bibliogr tabs

SINGH, R.N.P. and Singh, B.P.

Study in social participation of elected leaders. *quart J Local Self-Government Inst* 43(3) Ja-Mr'73 135-41 tabs

SINGH, R.P.
    See Singh, A.K. jt. auth.
____ and Ambastha, C.K.
Profession of farming and service in agriculture department : As block personnel see them. *Bihar Inform* 18(11)
16 Je'70 16-20 tabs
____ and Anil Kumar
Monograph of Bihar : A geographical study. Bharati
Bhawan. 1970, 193p. Review
nat Geographical J India 17(4) De'71 215
____ and Kumar, A.
Geomorphological evolution of stream order of the Topa
and Silphi basins in Ranchi. *nat Geographical J India* 15(1)
Mr'69 38-44 tabs figs

SINGH, Ramchandra Prasad
Sales tax in Bihar. *Bihar Inform* 18(20) 1 De'74 9-11

SINGH, Sant Lal
Towards a democratic administrative pattern for rural
development : A study of the Bihar Panchayat Smiti and
Zila Parishad Act, 1961. *mod Rev* 114(2) Ag'63 101-10

SINGH, T.P.
River valley projects. *ill Wkly India* 89(12) 24 Mr'69 22-23

SINHA, A.C.
The annual festivals among the Santals. *Vanyajati* 18(2)
Ap'70 84-98 bibliogr-ft-n
Leadership in a tribal society. *Man in India* 47(3) Jl-Se'67
222-27 bibliogr

SINHA, Anil Kumar
Bhola Paswan fall ascribed to Adivasi politics. *Janata*
24(32) 31 Ag'69 7+

SINHA, Anjani K.
Have UF Government failed in Bihar? *Mainstream* 6(46)
13 Jl'68 29-32
Must mistakes be repeated? *Mainstream* 8(20) 18 Ja'69
11-13

SINHA, D.P.
Culture change in an intertribal market. Asia. 1968,
xvi, 117p. Rs 25 Review
Eastern Anthropologist 22(1) Ja-Ap'69 132-33; *econ and
Political Wkly* 4(21) 24 My'69 873-77; *J soc Res* 11(2)
Se'68 163-64; *Man in India* 50(4) Oc-De'70 425-26

Innovation, response and development in Banari. *Man in India* 48(3) Jl-Se'68 225-43 tab bibliogr-ft-n

The Phariya in an intertribal market. *econ and Political Wkly* 2(31) 5 Ag'67 1373-78 bibliogr-ft-n

Processes of cultural change at the Banari inter-tribal market. *Tribe* 6(3) De'69 17-24

Socio-cultural implications of economic development in Banari : The case of Birhor resettlement. *Eastern Anthropologist* 20(2) My-Ag'67 109-32 bibliogr-ft-n

SINHA, G.P.

The pattern of industry. *ill Wkly India* 89(12) 24 Mr'68 14-15

SINHA, Indradeep

Bihar : Decisive battle ahead. *New Age* 22(39) 29 Se'74 1+

Bihar election scene : Struggle for Left democratic Front. *New Age* 16(50) 15 De'68 5+

The Bihar experience. *Link* 10(25) 26 Ja'68 34-41

Bihar's urgent needs; interview. *Link* 9(35) 9 Ap'67 24-25

Forward to Left-democratic Front in Bihar. *New Age* 16(33) 18 Ag'68 12-13 ills

Hoarders' raj in Bihar : Curbs on stock holdings lifted, no price control. *New Age* 13(30) 25 Jl'65 16

JP unleashes civil war among students. *New Age* 22(31) 4 Ag'74 8

New crisis in Bihar Govt's land policy. *New Age* 10(27) 8 Jl'62 7+

Raja's blackmail bout fails : Bihar SVD victory. *New Age* 16(27) 7 Jl'68 1+

Under Bihar United Front : Struggle for agrarian reforms. *Mainstream* 6(25) 17 Fe'68 10-15

Will centre discharge its responsibility? *New Age* 15(19) 7 My'67 12

SINHA, J.B.P.

  See Pandey, J. jt. auth.

SINHA, J.K.P.

Emerging trends in Bihar politics. *Indian J Pol Sci* 34(4) Oc-De'73 471-81 tabs

SINHA, J.N.

Wheat revolution in Shahabad. *Bihar Inform* 18(16) 16 Se'70 4-5 Repr

See also Mehdi, S.G. jt. auth.

SINHA, K.R.P.

Powerloom : As a vital base for rural industrialisation. *Bihar Inform* 18(2) 26 Ja'70 29-30

SINHA, Kamala

The battle of Patna. *Janata* 29(41) 17 Nv-24 Nv'74 16-17

SINHA, L.P.

Caste-based politics of opportunism. *Link* 12(1) 15 Ag'69 62-65

Kaleidoscopic change. *Link* 13(1) 15 Ag'70 59-63

SINHA, M.P

Bihar BKD group replaces. *TI* 2 Mr'69 9 : 4

Political and economic in Bihar. *AICC econ Rev* 19(11-13) 10 Ja'68 98-99

See also Mandal, S.C. jt. auth.

SINHA, Mahamaya Prasad

Famine under control; an interview. *Yojana* 11(9) 14 My'67 2-4+

SINHA, Manju

Changing agricultural income in Bihar. *Commerce (Suppl)* 127(3263) 17 Nv'73 75-76

SINHA, N.P.

Upgrading of skills : More rural artisans being trained. *Yojana* 6(15) 5 Ag'62 48-49

SINHA, Naval Kishore

Governors' functions as the Chancellor of the universities : A case study in Bihar during the period 1952-60. *Indian J Pol Sci* 23(1) Ja-Mr'62 72-82 bibliogr-ft-n

SINHA, P N.

Scope for agro-based industries. *Commerce (Suppl)* 127(3263) 17 Nv'73 27-29

SINHA, Pabitra Bhaskar

Development of the mineral industries of Bihar : 1833-1918. *J Historical Res* 16(1) Ag'73 74-86 ft-n

SINHA, R.C.

Attitude of students toward world mindedness. *J Psychol Res* 14(1) Ja'70 22-27 tabs bibliogr

SINHA, R.K.

Finance Commission and grants-in-aid : The case of Bihar. *Commerce (Suppl)* 127(3263) 17 Nv'73 67-69

SINHA, R.P. and Anil Kumar

Silk industry in Bhagalpur. *Deccan Geographer* 9(2) Jl-De'71 205-16 tabs maps bibliogr

SINHA, R.P.N.

Fairs and festivals. *ill Wkly India* 89(12) 24 Mr'68 42-44 ills

SINHA, R.T.

Opportunities of development. *Link* 7(23) 17 Ja'65 23-24

SINHA, Rajkishore

Agriculture in Bihar and the nationalised commercial banks. *Bihar Inform* 18(10) 1 Je'70 5-6 bibliogr-ft-n

Rural electrification and industrial development of North Bihar. *Bihar Inform* 18(12) 1 Je'70 8+

Rural electrifications and employment with special reference to Bihar. *Bihar Inform* 18(5) 16 My'70 9-11

State undertakings in Bihar and their profitability. *Bihar Inform* 18(8) 1 My'70 1-4

SINHA, Ram Narain

Bihar tenantry (1783-1833). People's Pub H. 1968, xii, 190p. Rs 20 Review
Indian econ soc Hist Rev 8(4) De'71 463-65; *Indica* 8(2) Se'71 122-24

SINHA, Ramdulari

Tourism in Bihar. *Link* 14(46) 25 Je'72 39-40

SINHA, S.C. and others

The concept of Diku among the tribes of Chotanagpur. *Man in India* 49(2) Ap-Je'69 121-38 bibliogr-ft-n

SINHA, S.P.

Birsa Bhagwan : The patriot. *Bihar Inform* 18(14) 15 Ag'70 38-40

Food policy and its administration in Bihar. *Mainstream* 6(42) 15 Je'68 19-22

———— and Jha, M.N.

Development of fisheries—A study of the fisherman cooperative societies in the district of Darbhanga, Bihar. *Indian J agric Econ* 23(4) Oc-De'68 243-47 tabs

———— and Verma, Biony Nath

An integrated development planning for a backward area of a backward district in Bihar. *Indian J agric Econ* 28(4) Oc-De'73 53-54

A study of agricultural production pattern in Bihar (A demand and supply analysis). *Indian J agric Econ*   27(4) Oc-De'72   143-46   tabs

A study of input (fertilizers) condition and marketing mechanism in the district of Saharsa, Bihar. *Indian J agric Econ* 28(4)   Oc-De'73   154-55

A study of the level of real earnings of agricultural worker in Bihar 1961-70. *Indian J agric Econ* 29(3) Jl-Se'74 70-71

SINHA, Surajit
Levels of economic initiative and ethnic groups in Pargana Barabham. *Eastern Anthropologist* 16(2) My-Ag'63 65-74

Space, time and ethnicity : Field study among the Bhumji of Barabhum. *J Indian anthrop Soc* 9(2) Oc'74   155-62 bibliogr

SINHA, Surendra Prasad
Processing industries and their role in a rural economy; a case study. *AICC econ Rev* 18(23) 15 Je'67 23-25+ tabs

―――― and Jha, Modnath
Labour market in rural Darbhanga. *Khadi Gramodyog* 18(6) Mr'72   391-94   tabs

SINHA, U.N.
Bihar State Agro-Industries Development Corporation. *Commerce (Suppl)* 127(3263) 17 Nv'73   63-67

SINHA, V.N.P.
See Gauntia, R. jt. auth.

SIVMURTISIMHA, Vatsa
*Bihar ki lok kathaem. Atmaram. Pt. 2. 1961, vi, 52p. ills Rs 1.50

SMALLPOX
Criminal neglect by paramedical staff. *TI* 18 Ag'74 1 : 1-2+

Dread disease; editorial. *TI* 30 Je'74 4 : 1

8,000 small-pox deaths in Bihar. *TI* 31 My'74 1 : 6-8+

Shameful; editorial. *TI* 17 Je'74   4 : 2

Shitala Mata ki jai ho; editorial. *Janata* 29(24) 21 Jl'74 1

Smallpox scourge in Bihar : A belated compaign. Jitendra Singh *TI* 2 Jl'74   4 : 7-8

Smallpox scourge in Bihar : A story of prolonged neglect. Dileep Padgaonkar *TI* 8 Jl'74 4 : 3-5

Smallpox.   *soc Welfare*   22(1)   Ap'75   31-34

25,000 small-pox deaths in Bihar alone.   *People's Democracy*
10(30)   28 Jl'74   3+

SMALL-SCALE industries

Bihar's poor industrial performance highlighted.   *TI*
17 Ja'69   9 : 5-6

Small industries in Bihar : Immense scope for growth.
J.S. Das   *Bihar Inform*   16(12)   1 Jl'68   3-5

Upgrading of skills : More rural artisans being trained.
N.P. Sinha   *Yojana*   6(15)   5 Ag'62   48-49

SOCIAL conditions

Impact of the struggle for freedom on the socio-economic
structure in Bihar. Sachchidananda   *Bihar Inform* 18(14)
15 Ag'70   56-59

*Social economic survey of Bihar city and Bairagarh. P.C.
Malhotra. Asia. 1964, 235p. Rs 25

Social implications of industrialisation in tribal Bihar. L P.
Vidyarthi *Anthropologist (Special Number)* 2 1969 37-52 ft-n

*Socio-economic survey of the workers in the coal mines
of India, with particular reference to Bihar. Virendra Lal
Srivastava. Scientific bk Ag. 1970, 643p. Rs 42

    See also

Caste

Cost and standard of living

Jamshedpur—Social conditions

Purulia—Social conditions

_____ : History

The mode of approach of the Mithila Smartas to various
social problems. Joyedeva Ganguly Shastri   *J Bihar Res
Soc (Sec III)*   48 Ja-De'62   34-49   bibliogr-ft-n

Social changes in Bihar in the second half of the 19th century. Surendra Gopal   *Man in India*   47(2)   Ap-Je'67
81-91   bibliogr

*Socio-religious, economic and literary condition of Bihar
(from ca. 319 A.D. to 1000 A.D.). Bhagvatisaran Varma.
Munshiram. 1962, xii, 209p. 36 pls bibliogr 24.5cm.
Rs 24

SOCIAL life and customs

Small town stories. Hamdi Bey. Barua Agency. Rs 22
Review
TI   30 Mr'75   8 : 4-5

See also

Marriage customs and rites

SOCIAL policy

Programme of the non-Congress government (Documents). *United Asia* 19(2) Mr-Ap'67 133-35

SOCIOLOGY, Rural

Notes on a method of studying rural society. Kumarananda Chattopadhyay and Suraj Bandyopadhyay   *Man in India* 42(3) Jl-Se'62 206-16 bibliogr-ft-n tabs

SOHANI, S.V.

Soc-Called Bihar stone pillar inscription of Shandagupta. *J Bihar Res Soc* 49 Ja-De'63 170-77 bibliogr-ft-n

SONARKAR, Sudhir

Six blind men. *econ and Political Wkly* 9(52) 28 De'74 2136-37

SRIVASTAV, Srinathprasad

*The Bihar gram cutcherry rules, 1962, with short notes and comments. Rung Bahadur Singh. 1962, iv, 40p. 22cm. Rs 2

*The Bihar panchayat raj (amendment and validating) Act, 1961 (Bihar Act viii of 1962) supplement to the spot-light on the Bihar Panchayat Raj Act, 1947. Rung Bahadur Singh. 1962, ii, 22p. 22cm.

*Bihar survey manual. Shri Prakash Pub. 1961, iv, 50p. Rs 5

*Spot-light on the Bihar Panchayat Raj Act 1947 (Bihar Act xxi of 1959) comments, comparative study and latest case laws up to Dec. 1, 1960. Shri Prakash Pub. 1960, xii, 163p. Rs 10

*Tenancy restriction on protected tenants. Rung Bahadur Singh. 1962, iv, 35p. 22cm. Rs 3

SRIVASTAVA, Dru and others

Short-term credit and farm productivity in an I.A.D.P. district. *Kurukshetra* 18(2) Nv'69 5-6

SRIVASTAVA, G.P.L.

Inter-block variations in family planning achievements. *J Family Welfare* 20(4) Je'74 34-42 tabs bibliogr

   See also Mathur, B.L. jt. auth.

SRIVASTAVA, L.R.N.

The role of education in modernization of Chotanagpur. *Indian educ Rev* 6(1) Ja'71 162-82 bibliogr

SRIVASTAVA, M.L.

Some aspects of fertility in a social group of India. *J soc Res* 12(2) Se'69 61-70 bibliogr tabs

SRIVASTAVA, Nagendra Mohan Prasad

Militant nationalism in Bihar (1900-1920). *Mainstream* 10(48) 29 Jl'72 35-39 bibliogr

SRIVASTAVA, S.S.

Bihar take the people's struggle forward. *People's Democracy* 10(14) 7 Ap'74 12

Champaran peasants' growing struggle : A serious challenge to Bihar U.F. government. *People's Democracy* 4(25) 23 Je'68 5+

SRIVASTAVA, Virendra Lal

*Socio-economic survey of the workers in the coal mines of India, with particular reference to Bihar. Scientific bk Ag. 1970, 643p. Rs 42

STATISTICS

*Bihar statistical handbook, for 1961. Bihar, Statistics (Directorate of). 1965.

*Bihar through figures. Bihar, Statistics (Directorate of). 1962, xiv, 114p.

STONE age

A study in the techniques of the neolithic bone tool making at Chirand and their probable uses. Lala Aditya Naraian *J Bihar Res Soc* 58(1-4) Ja-De'72 1-24 figs bibliogr

A technical study of some prehistoric potsherds. Alaknanda Ray and Gautamsankar Ray *Man in India* 43(2) Ap-Je'63 147-54 bibliogr

STRIKES

Bihar MLA's hunger-strike. K. Gopalan *New Age* 12(33) 16 Ag'64 10

Bihar presents a good record. *New Age* 12(36) 6 Se'64 3 ills

See also

Trade unions

____ : Coal miners

Coal miners resist owners' repression. Kalyan Roy *New Age* 15(19) 7 My'67 6

United strike against wage-cut in BSP mine. Prakash Roy *New Age* 15(25) 18 Je'67 7

_____ : Engineering workers

Engineering worker' struggle. *Link* 12(18) 14 De'69 14

Huge avoidable loss. *Capital* 164(4096) 15 Ja'70 84-85

Jamshedpur engg. workers strike for wage-rise. *People's Democracy* 5(48) 30 Nv'69 11

The Jamshedpur engineering workers strike in retrospect. *Indian Worker* 18(16-17) 26 Ja'70 6-7

Jamshedpur strike : What were the facts? V.N. Kishore *Janata* 15(5) 22 Fe'70 14

More than prestige; editorial. *econ and Political Wkly* 5(2) 10 Ja'70 33

_____ : Mining engineers

Mining engineers' strike. *Link* 7(13) 8 Nv'64 13

_____ : Teachers

Bihar secondary teachers on strike. *New Age* 19(16) 18 Ap'71 16

Bihar teachers' strike and after. Girish Misra and Braj Kumar Pandey *Mainstream* 7(35) 3 My'69 34-35

Falling standards. *Commerce* 116(2973) 27 Ap'68 1155-56

General strike unites Bihar teachers. Wasi Ahmad *New Age* 16(17) 28 Ap'68 3

Lathi charge on teachers in Patna jail. *TI* 10 Se'72 1 : 7-8+

Massive demonstration by Bihar teachers. *New Age* 16(13) 31 Mr'68 12

Unprecedented strike by Bihar teachers. *New Age* 16(13) 31 Mr'68 12

STUDENT unrest

CRP and BSF are drafted as violence spreads in Bihar. *TI* 9 Se'72 4 : 6+

Part of larger political plan. Janardan Thakur *econ and Political Wkly* 7(39) 23 Se'72 1964-65

Trifles that led to in Patna. *TI* 9 Se'72 9 : 1-2

Worsening mess; editorial. *TI* 9 Se'72 4 : 1

STUDENTS

Dependence proneness and preceived problems of adjustment. J. Pandey and J.B.P. Sinha *J Psychol Res* 12(3) Se'68 104-10

A study of the effect of economic status on students, attitude towards family planning. C P. Thakur and Manju Thakur *Indian J appl Psychol* 9(2) Jl'72 83-85 tabs bibliogr-ft-n

SUGAR industry and trade

Bihar continues to be backward. *Eastern Econ* 51(4) 26 Jl'68 235-41 tabs

Sahu-Jain game. *Link* 11(11) 27 Oc'68 13-14

'Shifting' crisis. *Commerce* 115(2955) 30 De'67 1543-44

Sugar industry in Bihar. A.V. Ambastha *AICC econ Rev* 20(1) 15 Jl'68 7-10 tabs

SUGARCANE

Acreage response of sugarcane in factory areas of North Bihar. Dayanatha Jha *Indian J agric Econ* 25(1) Ja-Mr'70 79-91 tabs bibliogr-ft-n

Cobweb phenomenon and fluctuations in sugarcane acreage in North Bihar. Dayanatha Jha and C.C. Maji *Indian J agric Econ* 26(4) Oc-De'71 415-21 fig

SUNDARARAMAN, K.

Industrial awakening in Bihar. *Eastern Econ* 40(22) 7 Je'63 1313-14

SUPPLY and Commerce Department

Important activities of the Supply and Commerce Department, Bihar. *Bihar Inform* 17(5) 16 Mr'69 16-20

SURANA, Pannalal

Socialists and the Bihar movement. *Janata* 29(28) 15 Ag'74 33-35

SURENDRA GOPAL

Social changes in Bihar in the second half of the 19th century. *Man in India* 47(2) Ap-Je'67 81-91 bibliogr

SURENDRA MOHAN

Consequences of the Bihar upsurge. *Janata* 29(13) 5 My'74 17-18

People's struggle without precedent. *Janata* 29(28) 15 Ag'74 21-23

Radical alternative and the Bihar struggle. *Janata* 29(31) 15 Se'74 5-6

SURESH SINGH

The Haribaba movement in Chotanagpur 1331-32. *J Bihar Res Soc* 49 Ja-De'63 284-96

SURESH SINGH, K.

Industrial development. *Commerce (Suppl)* 117(3263) 17 Nv'73 41-44

SURSAND : Communal riots

When Congressmen and communists stirred the communal cauldron. *Organiser* 21(14) 12 Nv'67 16

SUSHMA NAND

Some common information about family planning. *Bihar Inform* 17(20) 1 De'69 8-9

SWAMY, Roxna S.

People's administration already functioning in three distircts. *Organiser* 28(17) 7 De'74 7+

SWATANTRA Party : Bihar unit

Bihar state unit evaporates in thin air : Swatantra Party was Raja Ramgarh Party. *Organiser* 18(2) 24 Ag'64 15

Bihar unit of Swatantra Party; letter to the editor. *Swarajya* 9(11) 12 Se'64 23

TALES

*Kar bhala hoga bhala. Vinod Bhagvancandra. Sasta Sahitya Mandal. 1960.

TANABHAGATS, The

The Tana Bhagats. S.K. Chandhoke *Vanyajati* 19(2-3) Ap-Jl'71 81-94 bibliogr

TAXATION

Not only repression, more taxes in Bihar. K. Gopalan *New Age* 13(43) 24 Oc'65 10

_____ : Law

*Commentary on the law of excise in Bihar and Orissa. J.P. Bhatnagar. Ashoka Law H. 282p. Rs 12.50

TEACHERS

Bihar teachers plan satyagraha in March. K. Gopalan *New Age* 13(9) 28 Fe'65 6

Bihar teachers win demands. K. Gopalan *New Age* 19(20) 16 My'71 7

Dissatisfied teachers. *Link* 9(8) 2 Oc'66 20

A study of relationship between neuroticism and job satisfaction in school teachers. S.G. Mehdi and J.N. Sinha *Indian J appl Psychol* 8(1) Ja'71 46-47 bibliogr-ft-n

TEMPLE architecture

An unfinished rekha deal of Purulia. Adris Banerji *J Asiatic Soc (Bengal) (IV)* 7(3-4) 1965 163-66 bibliogr-ft-n

An unfinished rekha deal of Purulia. R. Nath *Marg* 22(2) Mr'69 2-23 ills

TEMPLES

Some post-Muslim temples of Bihar. Adris Banerji *J Asiatic Soc (Bengal)* 4(2) 1962 63-70 pls

Temples in Chotanagpur. P.C. Roy Choudhury *mod Rev* 121(2) Fe'67 137-38

See also

Visnupada temple

THAKAR, Jai Narain

Silk industry in Bihar. *J Bihar Res Soc* 58(1-4) Ja-De'72 285-313 tabs bibliogr-ft-n

THAKUR, C.P.

Competitive unionism in a new industrial centre. *Indian J industr Relations* 4(1) Jl'68 89-104 tab bibliogr

_____ and Thakur, Manju

A study of the effect of economic status on students, attitude towards family planning. *Indian J appl Psychol* 9(2) Jl'72 83-85 tabs bibliogr-ft-n

THAKUR, Janardhan

Operation 'total revolution.' *econ and Political Wkly* 10(8) 22 Fe'75 344-45

Part of larger political plan. *econ and Political Wkly* 7(39) 23 Se'72 1964-65

THAKUR, Manju

See Thakur, C.P. jt. auth.

THAKUR, S.N.

Rural labour market (Based on a study conducted in the district of Darbhanga, Bihar 1954-64). *Indian J agric Econ* 25(3) Jl-Se'70 65-66

THAKUR, S.P.

Industrial policy for fifth plan. *Commerce (Suppl)* 127(3263) 17 Nv'73 77-78

THAKUR, Upendra

Sanskrit learning in Mithila under the Khandavala dynasty. *J Bihar Res Soc (Sec III)* 48 Ja-De'62 90-104

Socio-economic life in Mithila under the Khandavalas. *J Bihar Res Soc (Sec III)* 48 Ja-De'62 64-89 ft-n

THAKUR PRASAD

BJS opposes communist tampering with Bihar Land Ceiling Act, 1961. *Organiser* 21(13) 5 Nv'67 7

BJS performance in Bihar poll. *Organiser* 22(28) 22 Fe'69 16+

THAPAR, Romesh

No way to govern. *econ and Political Wkly* 9(17) 27 Ap'74 657-58

TIWARY, K.N.

Planning at the state and district levels. *J nat Acad Adm* 15(4) Oc-De'70 145-54 bibliogr-ft-n

TOOFAN, Brij Mohan

The prince saviour of democracy. *Janata* 29(28) 15 Ag'74 17-21

TOPNO, Sem

Role of religion in the culture change of the tribes of Chotanagpur. *Vanyajati* 17(1) Ja'69 5-8 bibliogr

TOURIST trade

Tourism in Bihar. Ramdulari Sinha *Link* 14(46) 25 Je'72 39-40

What Bihar offers to tourists. Umanath *Bihar Inform* 18(16) 16 Se'70 6-8; *Foreign Trade of India* 26 Ag'65 50-51

TRADE unions

Big business mounts offensive; factional feuds beset INTUC. Satish Loomba *New Age* 13(8) 21 Fe'65 5

Competitive unionism in a new industrial centre. C.P. Thakur *Indian J industr Relations* 4(1) Jl'68 89-104 tab bibliogr

Outsiders in the labour unions in Bihar (a survey of outside leaders in the labour unions in the state of Bihar). R.C. Singh *Indian J Lab Econ* 9(4) Ja'67 532-44 bibliogr tabs

Trade unions must join the struggle. Hans Raj Gulati *Janata* 29(39) 10 Nv'74 5

_____ : History

A study of trade unions in Bihar. B.N. Shukla *Indian J Lab Econ* 11(3-4) Oc'68-Ja'69 C165-C76 tabs bibliogr-ft-n

Transport and accessibility in lower Ghaghara Gandak Doab. Rama Shanker Lal *Deccan Geographer* 7(1) Ja-Je'69 14-34 bibliogr fig tab

TRIBES

Adibasi 'Handia' beverage. Satya Prakash Gupta *Adibasi* 12(1-4) Ap'70-Ja'71 123-26 bibliogr

The Adivasi problem in Bihar. Binodananda Jha *Link (Annual Number)* 5(1) 15 Ag'62 39

Adivasis on the march. *soc Welfare* 20(3) Je'73 8-9

Adivasis on war path. *econ and Political Wkly* 3(26-28) Jl'68 977

Aspects of tribal labour force in Chotanagpur. L.P. Vidyarthi *Tribe* 6(3) De'69 54-62

The concept of Diku among the tribes of Chotanagpur. S.C. Sinha and others *Man in India* 49(2) Ap-Je'69 121-38 bibliogr-ft-n

Creating economic opportunities for the tribals in Bihar. *Capital* 174(4357) 3 Ap'75 502

Culture change in an intertribal market. D.P. Sinha. Asia. 1968, 112p. Rs 25 Review
Eastern Anthropologist 22(1) Ja-Ap'69 132-33; *J soc Res* 11(2) Se'68 163-64; *Man in India* 50(4) Oc-De'70 425-26

*Culture change in tribal Bihar, Munda and Oraon. Sachchidananda. Bookland. 1964, ii, 158p. Rs 12

Explosive situation in adivasi areas of Bihar. K. Gopalan *New Age* 16(25) 23 Je'68 8-9

Grim poverty cause of tribal unrest. *TI* 27 My'75 5 : 6

The Haribaba movement in Chotanagpur 1331-32. Suresh Singh *J Bihar Res Soc* 49 Ja-De'63 284-96

Impact of Brahminical culture on the tribes of Chotanagpur : IND festival—A case study. Pashupati Prasad Mahato *Folklore* 13(11) Nv'72 452-60 bibliogr

Impact of industrialization on Bihar tribes. Sachchidananda *Cultural Forum* 7(1-2) Ap'65 20-24

Leadership in a tribal society. A.C. Sinha *Man in India* 47(3) Jl-Se'67 222-27 bibliogr

Man and forest in Chotanagpur. Binay Kumar Rai *Vanyajati* 16(3) Jl'68 85-92

Material base of Santhal movement. *econ and Political Wkly* 10(11) 15 Mr'75 464-65

Needed urgent research for the fifth five-year plan for the tribal Bihar. L.P. Vidyarthi *Vanyajati* 21(1) Ja'73 4-14 tab bibliogr appdx

New stirringism adivasi politics. *Mainstream* 6(47) 20 Jl'68 25-28

Processes of cultural change at the Banari inter-tribal market. D.P. Sinha *Tribe* 6(3) De'69 17-24

The role of education in modernization of two tribes of Chotanagpur. L.R.N. Srivastava *Indian educ Rev* 6(1) Ja'71 162-82 bibliogr

Role of religion in the culture change of the tribes of Chotanagpur. Sem Topno *Vanyajati* 17(1) Ja'69 5-8 bibliogr

S.C. Roy's approach to the study of the tribal people in Chotanagpur. R.M. Sarkar *Vanyajati* 20(3-4) Jl-Oc'72 122-27

Social implications of industrialisation in tribal Bihar. L.P. Vidyarthi *Anthropologist (Social Number)* 2 1969 37-52 ft-n

Socio-cultural implications of industrialisation in India : A case study of tribal Bihar. L.P. Vidyarthi. Ranchi Univ. 1971, 540p. Rs 60 Review *Eastern Anthropologist* 26(3) Jl-Se'73 296-99

Stir among adivasis. *Link* 10(45) 16 Je'68 16-17

Tana Bhagat movement. Subhash Chandra Sarker *mod Rev* 130(1) Ja'72 22-26

The Tana Bhagats of Chota Nagpur. S.K. Chandhoke *Vanyajati* 20(3-4) Jl-Oc'72 128-44 bibliogr

Tribal culture. Sachchidananda *Marg* 20(1) De'66 55-60 ills

Tribal economy in Bihar. Sachchidananda *Commerce (Suppl)* 127(3263) 17 Nv'73 83-85

Tribal education in Bihar. Sachchidananda *Vanyajati* 12(1) Ja'64 3-6

Tribal leadership in Bihar. Sashishekhar Jha *econ and Political Wkly* 3(15) 13 Ap'68 603-08

*Tribal village in Bihar. Sachchidananda. Munshiram. 281p. Rs 24

Two tribal co-operatives. *mod Rev* 112(6) De'62 479-81

Why the tribal unrest. *Commerce* 117(3004) 30 Nv'68 1133

   See also

Bhumji

Kharia, The

Pahariyas, The

Tanabhagats, The

UJJAINIYAS, The

The account of the Ujjainiyas before their migration to Bihar. Dasharatha Sharma *J Bihar Res Soc* 49 Ja-De'63 197-99

UMANATH

What Bihar offers to tourists. *Bihar Inform* 18(16) 16 Se'70 6-8; *Foreign Trade of India* 26 Ag'69 50-51

UNEMPLOYMENT

Neglect and lethargy. *Link* 13(16) 29 Nv'70 14-15

Rural electrification and employment with special reference to Bihar. Rajkishore Sinha *Bihar Inform* 18(5) 16 Mr'70 9-11

Unemployment survey. *Commerce* 126(3220) 20 Ja'73 90

UNEMPLOYMENT, Rural

Unemployment in rural areas of Palamau District (Bihar) : A case study in Hussainabad block. M.L. Singh *Indian J agric Econ* 27(4) Oc-De'72 190-98 tabs

UNIVERSITIES and colleges

Bihar universities; letter to the editor. *Link* 14(50) 23 Jl'72 3

Cesspools of unlearning in Bihar. N.K. Singh *Swarajya* 16(52) 24 Je'72 2-3

Improvement in Bihar versities. *Link* 14(43) 4 Je'72 25

    See also

Patna College, Patna

____ : Employees

Bihar universities face crisis-staff on strike. K. Gopalan *New Age* 17(7) 27 Ap'69 4

UNIVERSITY of Patna : Students

Attitude of students towards world mindedness. R.C. Sinha *J Psychol Res* 14(1) Ja'70 22-27 bibliogr tabs

UPPAL, Hari

Folk dances of Bihar. *ill Wkly India* 89(11) 17 Mr'68 22-25 ills

URBAN property

Bihar at last moves on land question : Faces centre's obstruction on Tata zamindari—Willing to curb urban property holdings. *Link* 14(37) 23 Ap'72 20-21

Bihar Govt approves ceiling Ordinances. *TI* 31 Jl'71 1 : 2-5

Bihar ordinance ready to limit property holdings. K. Gopalan *New Age* 19(32) 8 Ag'71 3

URBAN sociology

*Towns of Uttar Pradesh, Bihar and Madhya Pradesh. Inst of Public Adm (Lucknow Univ). 139p. Rs 10

URBANISATION

Trends of urbanisation in Central Mithila. K.K. Lal Das *Mainstream* 11(45) 7 Jl'73 21-24 tabs

_____ : History

Trends in the urbanisation of the Chota Nagpur plateau. R. Gauntia and V.N.P. Sinha *Deccan Geographer* 7(2) Jl-De'69 117-28 tabs bibliogr

VALISIMHA, Devapriya

*A guide to Buddhagaya. Mahabodhi Soc of India. 2e. 1960, iv, 74p. Rs 1

VARMA, Bhagvatisaran

*Socio-religious, economic and literary condition of Bihar (from ca. 319 A.D. to 1000 A.D.). Munshiram. 1962, xii, 209p. 36 pls bibliogr 24.5cm. Rs 24

VARMA, Vishwanath Prasad

A study of the mid-term elections in Bihar 1969. Patna Univ. 318p. Rs 15 Review
South Asian Stud 6(1) Ja'71 88-90

VENKATESWARAN, R.J.

Bihar lacks infrastructure. *Eastern Econ* 59(7) 18 Ag'72 412-14 tabs

VERMA, Biony Nath

See Sinha, S.P. jt. auth.

VERMA, K.K. and Shukla, Prabha

Personality adjustment and family planning practices : A case-study of secondary school teachers. *J soc Res* 15(2) Se'72 115-19 tab

VERMA, Nawal Kishore Prasad

Civic administration of cantonments in Bihar. *quart J Local Self-Government Inst* 35(2) Oc-De'65 185-94

VERMA, V.P., ed.

A study of mid-term elections in Bihar 1969. Inst of Public Adm. (Univ of Patna). 1971, 318p. Rs 15 Review
Indian Political Sci Rev 6(2) Ap-Se'73 256-57

VIDYARTHI, L.P.

Aspects of tribal labour force in Chotanagpur. *Tribe* 6(3) De'69 54-62

The changing face of Ranchi. *ill Wkly India* 89(11) 17 Mr'68 43 ills

Ghagra—A village in Chotanagpur : Census of India-1961. The Registrar General of India (Monograph series No. 3). 1966, 158p. Rs 7.50 Review *Eastern Anthropologist* 21(2) My-Ag'68 247-48; *J Indian anthrop Soc* 2(2) Se'67 191-92; *Sociological Bull* 16(2) Se'67 107-09; *Voluntary Action* 10(1) Ja-Fe'68 23-24

Needed urgent research for the fifth five-year plan for the tribal Bihar. *Vanyajati* 21(1) Ja'73 4-14 tab bibliogr appdx

Social implications of industrialisation in tribal Bihar. *Anthropologist (Social Number)* 2 1969 37-52 ft-n

Socio-cultural implications of industrialisation in India. Ranchi Univ. 1971, 540p. Rs 60 Review *Eastern Anthropologist* 26(3) Jl-Se'73 296-99

_____ and Charley, Ganesh

*Bihar in folklore study; an anthology with a general editorial from Sankar Sengupta. Indian Pub. 1971, 312p. Rs 30

_____ and Sharma, P. Dash

A health survey of kamrr village, Ranchi. *J soc Res* 16(1) Mr'73 82-86 tabs appdx

VILLAGES

An analysis of occupational pattern in East Bihar villages. *Rural India* 32(4) Ap'69 97-100 tabs

Economic organisation of an Oraon village. A.K. Sengupta *Vanyajati* 13(2) Ap'65 41-45

Ghagra—A village in Chotanagpur : Census of India-1961. L.P. Vidyarthi. The Registrar General of India (Monograph series No. 3). 1966, 158p. Rs 7.50 Review *Eastern Anthropologist* 21(2) My-Ag'68 247-48; *J Indian anthrop Soc* 2(2) Se'67 191-92; *Sociological Bull* 16(2) Se'67 107-09; *Voluntary Action* 10(1) Ja-Fe'68 23-24

Motipur : A village outstanding. J. Dutt *Kurukshetra* 14(11) Ag'66 14-16 tabs

Some aspects of interactional pattern at village Kanchampura. Keshari N. Sahay *Indian Sociological Bull* 5(1) Oc'67 1-10

A whiff of change : Bihar.   Jitendra Singh   *TI (Mag)*
3 Ag'69   1 : 4-6

VIROTTAM, B.

The Nagbansis and the Choros. Munshiram. 1972, 224p.
Rs 29   Review
Indian Arch   22(1-2)   Ja-De'73   117-18

VISHNU PRASAD

Administrative tribunals in action—A study of administrative tribunals at the district level in Bihar.   Oxf-IBH.
vii, 240p.   Rs 32   Review
Commerce   130(3340)   24 My'75   793

VISNUPADA temple

An interesting stone panel from the Visnupada temple.
Bhagwant Sahai   *J Ganganath Jha Res Inst*   26(1-3)   Ja-Jl'70
709-15   bibliogr-ft-n

VISVANATHAPRASAD, *ed.*

*Magahi samskar-git. Bihar Rashtrabhasha Parishad. 1962,
xxvi, 308p. ills map 24.5cm. Rs 6 50

VIVEKANANDAN, B.

JP is pointing the way. *Janata*   29(28)   15 Ag'74   13-16

VOTING

Congress debacle in Bihar : Voting pattern in 1967.   *econ
and Political Wkly*   3(34)   24 Ag'68   1311-17   tabs

VYAS, A.C.

Export potential survey of Bihar.   *Foreign Trade Rev*   7(1)
Ap-Je'72   89-100   tabs

VYAS, U.K.

     See   Jaiswal, N.K. jt. auth.

WARIER, K.U.

Sahay's bid to prevent free poll. *New Age* 15(7)   12 Fe'67   3

WASI AHMAD

General strike unites Bihar teachers.   *New Age*   16(17)
28 Ap'68   3

WATER : Pollution

Need for water pollution control. P.S. Shaw   *Bihar Inform*
17(16)   16 Se'69   9-11

WATER supply

Urban water supply in Bihar through five-year plan.   U.D.
Chaubey   *Bihar Inform*   17(16)   16 Se'69   5-7

WHEAT

"A bumper harvest from wheat" in Bihar. A. Mahmood and Ram Kumar *Bihar Inform* 17(20) 1 De'69 25+

WILD life, Conservation of

Bihar bid to preserve wild life. S.P. Shahi *TI (Suppl)* 24 Nv'69 17 : 3-6

WITCHCRAFT

Witches, their training and modus operandi among the Oraons of Bihar. Pravangshu Sekhar Das Patnaik *Orissa Historical Res J* 12(2) 1964 109-12

WOMEN

Women in a coal-mining district. Indira Rothermund *econ and Political Wkly* 10(31) 2 Ag'75 1160-65 tabs bibliogr-ft-n

ZILLA Parishads

Towards a democratic administrative pattern for rural development : A study of the Bihar Panchayat Smiti and Zila Parishad Act, 1961. Sant Lal Singh *mod Rev* 114(2) Ag'63 101-10

LIST OF PERIODICALS INDEXED, WITH THEIR ABBREVIATION

AICC econ Rev : AICC Economic Review

All India Congress Committee, 7, Jantar Mantar Road, New Delhi

Adibasi

Tribal Research Bureau, Govt. of Orissa, Bhubaneswar-1, Orissa

Anthropologist

Deptt. of Anthropology, University of Delhi, Delhi-7

Assam Inform : Assam Information

Directorate of Information and Public Relations, Govt. of Assam, Shillong

Behavioural Sci and Community Development : Behavioural Science and Community Development

National Institute of Community Development, Rajendra Nagar, Hyderabad-30, Andhra Pradesh

Bengal Past & Present

Calcutta Historical Society, St. Paul's College, 33/1, Amherst Street, Calcutta-9

Bihar Inform : Bihar Information

Public Relations Department, Govt. of Bihar, Patna

Bull Cult Res Inst : Bulletin of the Cultural Research Institute

Cultural Research Institute, Scheduled Castes & Tribes Welfare Department, New Secretriat Buildings, 1st Floor, Block 'B' 1, Kiron Sankar Roy Road, Calcutta-700001, West Bengal

Call

Central Committee, Revolutionary Socialist Party, 780, Ballimaran, Delhi-6

Capital

Capital Private Ltd., Mission Row, Calcutta-1

Commerce

Brady House, Vir Nariman Road, Fort, Bombay-1, Maharashtra

Cultural Forum

Ministry of Education, E/3, Curzon Road, 'A' Barracks, New Delhi

Deccan Geographer
  Deccan Geographical Society, Subhadra Bhawan, 120-A, Nehru Nagar East, Secundrabad-26, Andhra Pradesh

Eastern Anthropologist
  Anthropology Department, Lucknow University, Lucknow, U.P.

Eastern Econ : Eastern Economist
  Eastern Economist Ltd., United Commercial Bank Building, Parliament Street, New Delhi

econ Affairs : Economic Affairs
  10 Galiff Street, Block 5, Scite 64, Calcutta-3, West Bengal

econ and Political Wkly : Economic and Political Weekly
  Sameksha Trust, Skylarke, 284, Frere Road, Bombay-400001, Maharashtra

econ Stud : Economic Studies
  Economic Studies and Journal Private Ltd., 2, Private Road, Calcutta-28, West Bengal

econ Wkly : Economic Weekly
  65, Apollo Street, Bombay-1, Maharashtra

Farmer and Parliament
  Farmers' Parliamentary Forum, 39, South Aweni, New Delhi

Folklore
  Indian Publications, 3, British Indian Street, Calcutta-1

Foreign Trade of India
  Directorate of Commercial Publicity, Ministry of Commerce, Udyog Bhavan, New Delhi

Foreign Trade Rev : Foreign Trade Review
  The Commercial Manager, Indian Institute of Foreign Trade, H-24, Green Park Extension, New Delhi-16

Gandhi Marg
  Gandhi Peace Foundation, 20-22, Rouse Avenue, New Delhi

Geographical Rev India : Geographical Review of India
  63-A, Hari Ghosh Street, Calcutta-6, West Bengal

Herald Libr Sci : Herald of Library Science
  C-1, Banaras Hindu University, Varanasi-5, U.P.

ill Wkly India : Illustrated Weekly of India
  The Times of India Press, P.O. Box No. 207, Bombay, Maharashtra

India quart : India Quarterly
  Asia Publishing House, Contractor Building, Nicol Road, Ballard Estate, Bombay-1, Maharashtra

Indian and Foreign Rev : Indian and Foreign Review
  Ministry of Information & Broadcasting, Govt. of India, New Delhi

Indian Architect
  B-50, Defence Colony, New Delhi-3

Indian Arch : Indian Archives
  National Archives of India, Janpath, New Delhi

Indian Cooperative Rev : Indian Cooperative Review
  72, Jorbagh, New Delhi

Indian econ soc Hist Rev : Indian Economic and Social History Review
  Delhi School of Economics, University Enclave, Delhi-7

Indian educ Rev : Indian Educational Review
  National Council of Educational Research & Training, Publication Unit, 71/1, Najafgarh Road, New Delhi-15

Indian Fin : Indian Finance
  6-2, Moria Street, Calcutta-17

Indian Fmg : Indian Farming
  Indian Council of Agricultural Research, New Delhi

Indian Geographical J : Indian Geographical Journal
  University of Madras, Centenary Buildings, Madras-5

Indian J Adult Educ : Indian Journal of Adult Education
  Indian Adult Education Association, 17-B, Indraprastha Marg, New Delhi-1

Indian J agric Econ : Indian Journal of Agricultural Economics
  Indian Society of Agricultural Economics, 46-48 Esp'anande Mansions, Mahatma Gandhi Road, Bombay-1, Maharashtra

Indian J appl Psychol : Indian Journal of Applied Psychology
  The Madras Psychology Society, Deptt. of Psychology, University of Madras, Madras-5

Indian J Commerce : Indian Journal of Commerce
  Department of Commerce, Lucknow University, Lucknow-7, U.P.

Indian J Econ : Indian Journal of Economics
  Department of Economics and Commerce, University of Allahabad, Allahabad

Indian J industr Relations : Indian Journal of Industrial Relations
    Shri Ram Centre for Industrial Relations and Human Resources, 5, Pusa Road, New Delhi-5

Indian J int Law : Indian Journal of International Law
    Indian Society of International Law, 7-8, Scindia House, New Delhi

Indian J Lab Econ : Indian Journal of Labour Economics
    Department of Economic, Lucknow University, Lucknow, U.P.

Indian J Pol Sci : Indian Journal of Political Science
    Department of Political Science, Utkal University, Vani Vihar, Bhubaneswar-4, Orissa

Indian J Publ Adm : Indian Journal of Public Administration
    Indian Institute of Public Administration, Indraprastha Estate, Ring Road, New Delhi

Indian J soc Res : Indian Journal of Social Research
    11-A, Ashok Colony, Begum Bagh, Meerut, U.P.

Indian J soc Wk : Indian Journal of Social Work
    Tata Institute of Social Sciences, Deptt. of Publications, Chembur, Bombay-71, Maharashtra

Indian Lab J : Indian Labour Journal
    Manager of Publications, Civil Lines, Delhi-6

Indian Librarian
    233, Model Town, Jullundur, Punjab

Indian Political Sci Rev : Indian Political Science Review
    C/o. The Dept. of Political Science, University of Delhi, Delhi-7

Indian Sociological Bull : Indian Sociological Bulletin
    Society Publication, Vashisht Printing Press, Model Town, Ghaziabad

Indian Worker
    Indian National Trade Union Congress, 17, Janpath, New Delhi

Indica
    St. Xavier's College, Calcutta-12, West Bengal

Interdiscipline
    The Sales Executive, The Gandhian Institute of Studies, P.B. 116, Rajghat, Varanasi-1, U.P.

Islamic Cult : Islamic Culture
  Opp. Osmania University, P.B. No. 171, Hyderabad-7, A.P.

J anthrop Soc Bombay : Journal of the Anthropological Society
  of Bombay
    Anthropological Society of Bombay, C/o K.P. Kama Orien-
    tal Library, 136, Apollo Street, Bombay-1, Maharashtra

J Asiatic Soc (Bengal) : Journal of Asiatic Society (Bengal)
  1, Park Street, Calcutta, West Bengal

J Asiatic Soc (Bombay) : Journal of Asiatic Society (Bombay)
  Town Hall, Bombay, Maharashtra

J Bihar Res Soc : Journal of Bihar Research Society
  Bihar Research Society, Museum Building, Patna

J Constitutional and Parliamentary Stud : Journal of Constitutional and Parliamentary Studies
    Institute of Constitutional and Parliamentary Studies, 19,
    Vitthalbhai Patel House, Rafi Marg, New Delhi-1

J Family Welfare : Journal of Family Welfare
    Family Planning Association of India, 1, Jeevan Udyog,
    Dadabhai Naoroji Road, Bombay-1, Maharashtra

J Ganganath Jha Kendriya Sk Vidyapeetha : Journal of the
  Ganganath Jha Kendriya Sanskrit Vidyapeehta
    Ganganath Jha Kendriya Sanskrit Vidyapeetha, Allahabad,
    U.P.

J Historic Res : Journal of Historical Research
  Ranchi

J Indian anthrop Soc : Journal of the Indian Anthropological
  Society
    Indian Anthropological Society, 35, Ballygunge Circular
    Road, Calcutta-19

J Indian Hist : Journal of Indian History
  University of Kerala, Trivandrum

J nat Acad Adm : Journal of National Academy of Administration See J Lal Bahadur Shastri nat Acad Adm
    National Academy of Administration, "Charles Villa",
    Mussoorie, U.P.

J orient Inst : Journal of Oriental Institute
  Oriental Institute, Station Road, Baroda, Gujarat

J orient Res : Journal of Oriental Research
  Kuppuswami Sastri, Research Institute, Mylapore,
  Madras-4

J Psychol Res : Journal of Psychological Research
> University Examination Hall, Marine, Madras-5

J soc Res : Journal of Social Research
> Council of Social and Cultural Research, Bihar and Deptt. of Anthropology, Ranchi University, Ranchi, Bihar

J soc Stud State Govts : Journal of the Society for Study of State Governments
> The Society for Study of State Governments Old D/4, Malaviyanagar, Varanasi-5, U.P.

Janata
> Praja Socialist Party of India, National House, 6, Tulloch Road, Apollo Bunder, Bombay-1

Khadi Gramodyog
> Erla Road, Ville Parle (West), Bombay-6

Kurukshetra
> Business Manager, Publications Division, Patiala House, New Delhi-1

Link
> United India Periodicals Ltd., Bahadur Shah Zafar Marg, New Delhi-1

Maha Bodhi
> 4/A, Bankim Chatterjee Street, Calcutta-12

Mainstream
> Perspective Publications (Pvt.) Ltd., 18, Ring Road, New Delhi-14

Man in India
> The Manager, Man in India Office, 18, Church Road, Ranchi, S.E. Rly., Bihar

Mankind
> 7, Gurdwara Rakabganj Road, New Delhi

Marg
> 34-38, Bank Street, Bombay, Maharashtra

mod Rev : Modern Review
> 77/2/1, Dharamtalla Street, Calcutta-13

Monthly Comm on Indian econ Conditions : Monthly Commentary on Indian Economic Conditions
> Indian Institute of Public Opinion (P) Ltd., 2-A, National Insurance Bldg., Parliament Street, New Delhi

nat Geographical J India : National Geographical Journal of
India
National Geographical Society of India, Banaras Hindu
University, Varanasi-5, U.P.

New Age
Communist Party of India, 7/4, Asaf Ali Road, New Delhi

Organiser
4132, Naya Bazar, Delhi

Orissa Historical Res J : Orissa Historical Research Journal
Superintendent of Archaeology and Museum, Bhubaneswar,
Orissa

Patna Univ J : Patna University, Journal
Assistant Registrar, Patna University, Patna-5

People's Democracy
West Bengal State Committee of the Communist Party of
India, 33, Alimuddin Street, Calcutta-16

Political and econ Rev : Political and Economic Review
7, Jantar Mantar Road, New Delhi

Political Sci Rev : Political Science Review
Dept. of Political Science, University of Rajasthan, Jaipur

Productivity
National Productivity Council of India, 38, Golf Links,
New Delhi-3

quart J Local Self-Government Inst : Quarterly Journal of the
Local Self-Government Institute
All-India Institute of Local Self-Government, 11, Horniman
Circle, Bombay-1, Maharashtra

Religion and Soc : Religion and Society
Christian Institute for the Study of Religion and Society,
P.O. Box 604, 17, Milliers Road, Bangalore-560006

Rural India
Ishwaradas Mansions, Nava Chowk, Bombay-7

Sankhya
204/1, Barrackpore Trunk Road, Calcutta-35

Seminar
Malhotra Building, Janpath, New Delhi

soc Action : Social Action
Indian Social Institute, Lodi Road, New Delhi-110003

soc Welfare : Social Welfare

    Central Social Welfare Board, Jeewan Deep, Parliament Street, New Delhi

Sociological Bull : Sociological Bulletin

    Department of Sociology, Delhi School of Economics, University of Delhi, Delhi-7

South Asian Stud : South Asian Studies

    South Asian Studies Centre, Deptt. of Political Science, University of Rajasthan, Jaipur

Southern Econ : Southern Economist

    33/5, Infantry Road, Bangalore-1

Swarajya

    Kalki Buildings, Chetput, Madras-31

TI : Times of India

    Times of India Press, Dadabhai Naoroji Road, Bombay-1

Thought

    Siddhartha Publications (P) Ltd., 35, Netaji Subhash Marg, Delhi-6

Tribe

    Tribal Research Institute and Training Centre, Ashok Nagar, Udaipur (Rajasthan)

United Asia

    12, Rampart Row, Bombay-1

Vanyajati

    Bharatiya Adamjati Sewak Sangh, New Link Road, Jhandewalan, New Delhi-1

Vidura

    Press Institute of India, Sapru House, Annex, Barakhamba Road, New Delhi

Voluntary Action

    Association of Voluntary Agencies for Rural Development, A-23, Kailash Colony, New Delhi-14

Weekend Rev : Weekend Review

    Times of India Press, Dadabhai Naoroji Road, Bombay-1

Yojana

    Publications Division, Government of India, New Delhi

LIST OF PUBLISHERS

A.N. Sinha Inst of Soc Stud. A.N. Sinha Institute of Social Studies, Patna, Bihar

Anand Prakash. Anand Prakash, Sahibganj, Bihar

Ashoka Law H. Ashoka Law House, Allahabad, Uttar Pradesh

*Asia. Asia Publishing House, Calicut Street, Ballard Estate, Bombay-1

Asiatic Soc. Asiatic Society, 1, Park Street, Calcutta-16

Atmaram. Atmaram and Sons, P.B. 1429, Daryaganj, Delhi-6

Barua Agency. Barua Agency, Dighall Pukhuripar, Gauhati (Assam)

*Bharati Bhawan. Bharati Bhawan, Exhibition Road, Patna-1, Bihar

*Bharatiya Adimjati Sevak Sangh. Bharatiya Adimjati Sevak Sangh, Thakkar Bapa Samarak Sadan, New Link Road, Jhandewalan, New Delhi-1

*Bihar, Publ Relations Dept. Bihar, Public Relations Department, Patna, Bihar

*Bihar, Statistics (Directorate of). Bihar, Statistics (Directorate of) Patna, Bihar

Bihar Rashtrabhasha Parishad. Bihar Rashtrabhasha Parishad, Patna-3

Bookland. Bookland Private Ltd., 1, Shankar Ghose Lane, Calcutta-6, West Bengal

CIRT. Central Institute of Research and Training in Public Cooperation, C-1/4, Safdarjang Development Area, Hauz Khas, New Delhi-16

*Chief Conservator of Forests. Chief Conservator of Forests, Government of Bihar, Patna, Bihar

Chowkhamba Sk. Chowkhamba Sanskrit. K37/99 Gopal Mandir Lane, P.B. 8, Varanasi-1, Uttar Pradesh

*Darbhanga Press Co. Darbhanga Press Co. Private Ltd., Darbhanga, Bihar

Granthamala Karyalaya. Granthamala Karyalaya, Patna-4, Bihar

India, Min of Home. Ministry of Home Affairs, New Delhi-1

*Indian Pub. Indian Publications, 3, British Indian Street, Calcutta-1

Indian Soc Inst. Indian Social Institute, New Delhi

*Indological bk House. Indological Book House, Varanasi

Inst of Public Adm. (Lucknow Univ). Institute of Public Administration, Lucknow University, Lucknow, U.P.

Inst of Public Adm. (Univ of Patna). Indian Institute of Public Administration, Patna University, Patna, Bihar

Jha, Laksminath. Laksminath Jha, Sarsib, Sarsib Pahi, Darbhanga, Bihar

K.P. Jayaswal Res Inst. K.P. Jayaswal Research Institute, Patna, Bihar

Mahabodhi Soc of India. Mahabodhi Society of India, 4/A, Bankim Chatterjee Street, Calcutta-12, West Bengal

*Malhotra, C.P. C.P. Malhotra, Patna, Bihar

Meenakshi. Meenakshi Prakashna, Begum Bridge, Meerut, Uttar Pradesh

*Mukhopadhyay. Firma K.L. Mukhopadhyay, 6/1a, Bancharam Akrur Lane, Calcutta-12, West Bengal

Munshiram. Munshiram Manohar Lal, 10B, Netaji Subash Marg, Post Box 1165, Nai Sarak, Delhi-6

*N.C.A.E.R. National Council of Applied Economic Research, Parsila Bhavan, 11, Indraprastha Estate, New Delhi

National Pub H. National Publishing House, 2/35, Ansari Road, Delhi-6; 26 A, Jawahar Nagar, Delhi-7

Oxf-IBH. Oxford and IBH Publishing Co, 17 Park Street, Calcutta-16, West Bengal; Oxford Building, N-88, Connaught Circus, New Delhi

Pahuja Brothers. Pahuja Brothers, Opp. Patna College, Patna 6 (Bihar)

*Panjab Univ. (Dept. of Economics). Panjab University, (Dept. of Economics), Chandigarh, Punjab

Patna College. Patna College, Patna, Bihar

Patna Univ Patna University (Dept. of Applied Economics and Commerce), Patna-4, Bihar

People's Pub H. People's Publishing House, Private Ltd., Rani Jhansi Road, New Delhi-55

Rachna. Rachna Prakashan, E-73, Greater Kailash, New Delhi-14

*Rajhans. Rajhans Publications, Rui Mandi, Sadar Bazar, Delhi-6

Ranchi Univ. Ranchi University, Ranchi, Bihar

Registrar General of India. See India, Min of Home

*Rung Bahadur Singh. Rungh Bahadur Singh, Mahalla Bindtoli, Arrah, Bihar

S. Chand. S. Chand and Co., (P) Ltd., Ram Nagar, New Delhi-55

*Sahitya Akad.   Sahitya Akademi, Rabindra   Bhavan, 35,
    Feroz Shah Road, New Delhi

Sampradayikta Viro Comm.   Sampradayikta Virodhi Commi-
    tee, New Delhi

Sasta Sahitya Mandal.   Sasta   Sahitya   Mandal,   Connaught
    Circus, New Delhi-1

*Scientific bk Ag. Scientific Book Agency, 103, Netaji Subhash
    Road, Calcutta-1,   West Bengal

Shanti Devi.   Shanti Devi, Madhipura, Bihar

Shri Prakash Pub.   Shri Prakash Publications,   Maulabagh,
    Mahabirsthan, Arrah, Bihar

Sindhu Pub.   Sindhu Publications Pvt Ltd.,   Hind   Rajasthan
    Chamber, 4th Floor 6 Oak Lane, Fort, Bombay-1

Super Bazar.   Super Bazar, New Delhi

*Vikas Maitri.   Vikas Maitri, Ranchi, Bihar

Vora. Vora and Co., Publishers Private Ltd., 3, Round
    Building, Bombay-2